The Power of Emotional Decision Making

Dr. David Hawkins
THE RELATIONSHIP DOCTOR

HARVEST HOUSE PUBLISHERS

EUGENE, OREGON

Cover by Koechel Peterson & Associates, Inc., Minneapolis, Minnesota

This book contains stories in which the author has changed people's names and some details of their situation in order to protect their privacy.

This book is not intended to take the place of sound professional psychological advice. Neither the author nor the publisher assumes any liability for possible adverse consequences as a result of the information contained herein.

THE POWER OF EMOTIONAL DECISION MAKING
Copyright © 2008 by David Hawkins
Published by Harvest House Publishers
Eugene, Oregon 97402
www.harvesthousepublishers.com

Library of Congress Cataloging-in-Publication Data
Hawkins, David, 1951-
The power of emotional decision making / David Hawkins.
    p. cm.
Includes bibliographical references.
ISBN-13: 978-0-7369-2142-8
ISBN-10: 0-7369-2142-7
1. Emotions—Religious aspects—Christianity. 2. Decision making—Religious aspects—Christianity.
I. Title.
BV4597.3.H39 2008
248.4—dc22

                                                                2007028421

Printed in the United States of America

08 09 10 11 12 13 14 15 16 / VP-SK / 11 10 9 8 7 6 5 4 3 2 1

To my two sons, Dr. Joshua Hawkins and soon-to-be Dr. Tyson Hawkins. Like my father and me, you guys turned out to be "emotional males," and I think that will serve you well.

Acknowledgments

The birth of a new book is exciting. All of these words represent hours of labor, both for the author and for many people behind the scenes who may never receive full appreciation.

I'm fortunate to have a team in place at this stage of my writing, a group who work tirelessly to assist me in collecting and sorting my thoughts, writing, editing, and finally promoting a book.

First, I thank the entire Harvest House Publishing team, beginning with Terry Glaspey, who encourages my writing and goes to bat for me with the Publishing Committee—sometimes again and again. I owe you big time, Terry.

And Gene Skinner, who edits many garbled phrases—"Did you really mean to say…?" and "Are you sure about that Scripture?" More often than not, he's caught some real mistakes. The ones not caught are my responsibility.

And then I have an incredible PR team who send me out, far and wide—and I do mean far and wide (whew!)—as the "media hound" they claim I am. You all mean the world to me.

I also thank my wonderful wife, Christie, who creates an encouraging, gracious, and loving space for me to write, and then reads the first crummy draft. Christie, as you read my latest chapter, I watch your gestures with eager anticipation and at times a bit of concern. Sometimes you smile, and I know I'm on the right track. Sometimes you groan, and I know I've used too many words in a story, put too many commas in a sentence, or drifted too far from the main theme of the chapter. Your incisive skills always greatly improved my work, and I thank you.

Next I thank Jim Lemonds, who edits my work as well. (My work sometimes needs lots of editing!) Jim, you've been an integral part of my team for years now, and I appreciate everything you do to make my work crisper, more powerful, and often less wordy.

I also thank those who have counseled with me professionally over the past 30-plus years. I consider myself a teacher of sorts, but you teach me during every session. Your stories, and the struggles they involve, are the reason I write.

Last, but certainly not least, I thank God for the opportunity to write. I am blessed beyond measure to be able to spend my time in this way.

Contents

Emotions:
Your Source of Energy and
Decision-Making Power

*What lies behind us and what lies before us are tiny
matters compared to what lies within us.*

OLIVER WENDELL HOLMES

As a man and his young son approached the checkout counter, the boy began tugging on his father's pants, reaching for the candy display and talking excitedly

"Daddy, I want some gum. You promised me some candy. Can I have one of these?" The boy became more animated, eyes big, hands grabbing for a candy bar and chewing gum.

At first the father seemed annoyed and simply scolded his son. "No, Jack," he impatiently replied, "I didn't promise you candy today. We've got to get home."

"But, Daddy," the boy continued louder, "you promised me something when we were home. Remember?" The boy began to whimper.

Then, in a moment of tenderness, the father reached down and touched his son gently on the shoulders. "You're right. I remember. I did promise you something, didn't I? Let's pick out something we can share together."

The boy beamed with excitement and pleasure, reaching immediately for a pack of gum. A crisis was averted.

Scenes like this occur daily. Everyday situations are rife with emotional energy—our own and that of those around us. Like the father in the above scene, we can harness our emotions, understand them, and direct them for positive outcomes. We can use emotional energy to make effective decisions.

In this book, you will learn to listen to your emotions and understand how they are vital sources of energy that can help you make good decisions in your everyday life. You will learn how you can also misunderstand or misdirect your emotions, creating further chaos and havoc in your life. You will see how emotions can be a powerful source of information and how you can use emotional decision making to create emotional well-being.

Moping About Milwaukee

As I was writing this book, a friend and colleague shared his own story that revealed the surprisingly powerful way emotions can either cause trouble or motivate positive change. Craig thought that he had resolved issues related to his first marriage, but his new wife, Jannine, unknowingly triggered a blast of memories and feelings that threatened the stability of their marriage.

Several months ago, Jannine told Craig they had been invited to Milwaukee to celebrate her brother's fiftieth birthday. Craig has always enjoyed Jannine's brother and sister-in-law, and he was excited to visit them and see their new loft condo in downtown Milwaukee. He envisioned a fun weekend in the city.

But recently, Jannine told Craig she would have to go to Milwaukee alone because the dates of their visit conflicted with an important convention Craig's employer wanted him to attend. This news caught Craig off guard, and he was surprised by the flood of emotions washing over him.

As Craig and Jannine ate dinner, he felt his mood slipping. He sensed Jannine's excitement at seeing her brother, and yet he felt abandoned. He told her he wanted her to be able to celebrate with her family. His head said this was a reasonable thing for her to do and something she would delight in. She would fly in with her older brother and sister-in-law for a surprise visit. Yet his words were hollow, and his gut told a much different story.

Jannine immediately noticed his disappointment.

"What's the matter, sweetie?" she asked.

"I don't really know. I guess I'm disappointed that I won't be making this trip with you. I suppose I'm also a little down about the fact that I'll be working while you're having fun in Milwaukee."

"You know I'd love for you to go too." She reached out, lovingly touched his arm, and smiled at him.

But her words and touch did not soothe his troubled spirit. In fact, he could barely hear her because of the clamoring in his mind. Suddenly, without warning, images flew into his brain. He was transported to another time and place. Tears filled his eyes.

He flashed back to 1999. He was alone in his living room, repeating a scene he'd lived out many times that year. Attempting to busy himself with reading a book, he anxiously watched the clock. Eight o'clock came and went, with no phone call from his wife, who was out with friends. Nine o'clock, and still no call. Nine thirty, and not a word. A cacophony of emotions—anger, resentment, confusion, and fear—rang in his brain. He was overcome by rejection and abandonment.

He was angry that she hadn't called—again—to tell him why she was late or when she'd be home. He was hurt that she refused to be held accountable to their marriage. He felt rejected, with no outlet for his emotions. He felt like a little boy waiting for his tardy parents to pick him up. What in the world could he do with these emotions?

"Are you okay?" Jannine said, her voice carrying him back to the present.

"No," he said. "I'm not okay, and I don't really know how to be okay. I shouldn't be reacting like this to your leaving, but I can't help it."

He shared with Jannine the story of how he had been left, evening after evening, wondering where his wife was spending her time, unable to confront her because she would become defensive, making matters worse. He told Jannine he had gathered a group of men from his church around him as a life-support network to help him manage his feelings. He also told Jannine that her trip to Milwaukee had awakened all those feelings.

"But that was then, and this is now."

"I know that in my mind, but in my heart, then is now."

He couldn't make sense out of his emotions. They were a jumbled mess inside his brain. Since emotions are "energy in motion," a lot of action was taking place in his head. He could imagine the Indianapolis Speedway in his brain, with different cars representing different emotions. In a pileup on turn seven, Anger collided with Hurt and Sadness, flipping over Guilt. Now, when he most needed a huge hug and reassurance from his new wife, he defiantly pulled away from her, his emotions skidding out of control.

Craig did not have a clue about how to deal with this situation. He wanted to tell Jannine not to go to Milwaukee, but that would certainly be selfish. He wanted a hug from her but had already pushed her away. He wanted to stop projecting yesterday's pain onto today's situation, but he didn't have enough control of his mind to do that.

He was a mess.

When they went to bed a short time later, Jannine moved close. But Craig turned away from her and prayed for sleep. He practiced breathing deeply to relax his tense muscles. He imagined Satan on one shoulder, shouting at him, "Push her away. She's hurt you." On the other shoulder was the Holy Spirit, saying, "Reach out to your wife. She loves you and will comfort you." The battle raged on for what seemed like hours, though it was actually only a few minutes.

Jannine would have loved for Craig to reach out to her. But pride got in his way.

Sleep finally came, but Craig was awakened an hour later, anxiety pulsing through his body, his thoughts racing. He was angry with his ex, still sad and hurt from the pain he had experienced and yet feeling guilty about the way he had treated Jannine.

Finally, he reached out and told Jannine he loved her. She took his hand and squeezed it. He was then able to fall back asleep.

Emotional Crisis or Opportunity

With the immediate crisis over, Craig wanted to move past the anguish he felt from what had happened years ago. He wanted, more than anything, to do as Jannine had previously asked: "Don't put onto me what belongs to her." Certainly this was fair. His old "stuff" didn't fit her or their relationship. But old emotions don't just settle into a nice, cozy place to sleep their lives away. They gurgle and grumble under the surface, erupting at the most inopportune times, clamoring for attention: "Deal with me now or deal with me later."

Craig's unruly emotions were demanding that he deal with them. He could try to ignore them, but he knew they would not go away. He had a decision to make. He could busy himself with projects and try to ignore this eruption of feelings. He could push the balloon of emotions back under the water and hope they would remain indefinitely. Or he could use this mini-crisis as an opportunity for change. He could acknowledge the emotional energy, embrace it, and make decisions that would be healthy for him and his relationship with Jannine.

He finally chose the latter. He decided to unwrap his feelings from years of rejection, abandonment, and divorce, and to inspect them as honestly as he could. He sat down with his trusted journal and wrote about the recent incident with Jannine and the feelings it had awakened from his past. His raw, unedited feelings flowed onto the page. He stopped insisting his emotions make sense from some preconceived point of view. Rather, he simply let them be, and then took notice. He was gentle with himself.

Emotions and Decisions

Having let the feelings come out onto the page, Craig was able to review them more clearly. He was able to make decisions about them—and that is the ultimate purpose of this book. He attempted, though somewhat feebly, to accept his feelings rather than stuffing them into a box and putting them away. He tried to let his emotions have their say.

Most of us have suspected our emotions and even labeled them as irrational, out of control, or selfish. We have often heard that emotions are questionable, untrustworthy, and fickle. That isn't necessarily so.

Although Craig's unruly emotions caused him fits one evening and he wounded his wife's feelings as a result, they did little damage in the long run. In fact, they were instructive. These feelings reminded him that he had some grief-related work to do. They told him again that unless he did that work, he would continue to overreact to other hurts and struggles. He decided to call me and ask me to help him process these emotions and to help him keep old emotions from spilling needlessly onto his new marriage.

This book invites you to become acquainted with a basic aspect of your personality—your emotions—and demonstrates several critical factors about them:

- Emotions are part of the heart of God. Jesus, God incarnate, experienced the full gamut of emotions and fully understands our emotional challenges.

- Emotions are energy in motion. If we deny them, we will intensify them.

- Embracing our emotions can help us live fuller, richer lives.

- Emotions can help us or hinder us as we listen for God's voice.

- Denying our emotions is often a very destructive process.

- We can learn not to be overcome by our emotions by discovering how to balance our emotional responses with intellectual decisions.

- Anger can empower us to change or tempt us to destroy.

- Resentment is the poison pill we ingest when we consider getting even with another person.

- Depression is often nothing more than anger turned inward.

- Envy can be a useful emotion that helps us determine what is missing in our lives.

- Grief is often the healing feeling.

- Delight can bring joy and gladness into our lives.

- We can learn to listen to our heart for a change.

Trusting Your Emotions

This book invites you to begin trusting your emotions and exploring creative ways to learn about this intimate aspect of your personality. Moreover, I invite you to examine how your emotions can be instructional—helping you settle old issues, make new decisions, and discover the heart of God. You *can* trust your emotions. Emotions are true and useful and can help you make decisions that will positively influence your life.

Emotions aren't always welcome visitors, as Craig discovered. Old, suppressed emotions of rejection and abandonment rose up to cloud his relationship with Jannine. Overwhelmed by these feelings, he was tempted to distrust them and to suppress them again. But he knew they would only resurface later, perhaps making another situation worse.

As he wrote in his journal, he began to understand that his feelings were at least partially legitimate even though they were remnants of his past. He knew he would be better off if he acknowledged his old pain and remembered that Jannine was not rejecting him. Though he was tempted to stifle his pain, he knew that doing so would be unwise.

Attempting to simply forget about our past or negate the power of our current emotions is one of the greatest mistakes we can make. We often try to relegate emotions to the back of the bus. Intellect is prized; emotions are undervalued. Rationality is trustworthy; emotions are fickle.

These generalizations don't serve us well. They create a schism between our mind and our heart, between our head and our gut-level emotions. Such a split often causes us great damage. Emotions, as I said, are energy in motion that cannot be simply dammed up. Even if we do succeed in damming them up, they will breach their banks at some time in the future.

To Be Fully Human

I struggle as much as the next person with unruly emotions. At times, I wish I had been created a stoic, unemotional male. Sometimes I blame my father, who is also an emotional male. Why couldn't I be a rugged John Wayne type, defended and tough-minded, letting every emotion roll off my back?

But that is not the case. I am an emotional man, and I need to deal with it. Perhaps you're reading this book because you too are an emotional person. You can take comfort in knowing that Jesus was also an emotional person. You will soon see that Jesus cried, became angry and righteously indignant, and felt discouragement. He experienced the full array of emotions.

At times I want to live from the neck up, but my emotions make me fully human—unruly though they may be. The fact that I can be hurt, feel confusion, and struggle with pain and loss makes me a fully dimensional individual. As much as I tell myself that I'd like to be a robot at times, that is not really my heart's desire.

Accepting and understanding our emotions helps us live fuller lives. Our feelings are a huge part of our functioning, so acquainting yourself with your own emotions and what they are saying to you is a big step toward living a fuller life. To learn to walk comfortably with your feelings is to access an abundance of knowledge. Further, God may speak to you through your emotions, making them an even richer source of understanding.

Perhaps you approach this book with a tendency to overreact to certain situations. This book will help you make sense of that behavior. If you are prone to feelings of anxiety or depression, it can help you work with your feelings more constructively, reducing the possibility of slipping back into a melancholy state. If you have issues with anger, you can learn to review the softer feelings lurking beneath the surface.

This undertaking can be richly rewarding. It can help you function more fully and enjoy a life in which your emotions serve you in making better, more godly decisions.

I invite you to join me as we discover how emotions are natural, God-given, and instructive in leading healthy, wholesome lives.

1

Emotions and the
Heart of God

The Holy Spirit is our harpist, and all strings
Which are touched in Love must sound.

Mechthild of Magdeburg

Creativity is an emotional act of the soul. Anyone who has painted a sunset, sculpted a statue, woven a tapestry, or written a poem knows that emotion and creativity are integrally interwoven. Creating without emotion is impossible.

In the beginning, God created the world, and "the morning stars sang together and all the angels shouted for joy" (Job 38:7). This is sheer exaltation.

A reading of the Genesis account of the creation story reflects a God who is intimately and joyfully involved in His creation. We read about His masterpiece coming together day after day, crowned by His creation of man.

In Genesis 2:2, we see God take a break from His work. I imagine Him scanning over His creative expression, smiling. We read in 1:31, "God saw all that he had made, and it was very good." And all the angels shouted for joy.

But some people may read the creation account and think God was distant and emotionless. "Let there be light," He said. "Let there be an expanse between the waters to separate water from water...Let the water under the sky be gathered to one place, and let dry ground appear."

The crisp style of the text may seem to imply that God was detached and uninvolved, but this is completely untrue. God was very involved, engaged with His creation, and emotionally connected to humanity. He even created man in His own image—a profound connection.

"By the seventh day God had finished the work he had been doing; so on the seventh day he rested from all his work. And God blessed the seventh day and made it holy, because on it he rested from all the work of creating what he had done" (Genesis 2:2-3).

Was God tired from all that creating He'd been doing? Did He need a break? Or instead, did He simply begin modeling a critical biblical concept of resting—taking a Sabbath rest from our work? We catch a glimpse into the heart of God regarding resting, and we see it repeated again and again throughout Scripture.

As the creation account unfolds, we see more and more similarities between humanity and God. It was not enough to create our magnificent earth and heavens. He decided to make man in His image. A short time later, He saw that Adam "had no suitable helper" and took a rib from Adam and created Eve. This is hardly an emotionless executive issuing blessings. This is a God intimately involved in His personal handiwork. He wants all of creation, including humankind, to experience fully blessed lives. In short, He cares.

But the pristine scene dramatically changes, and we can almost hear God groan after the first act of disobedience. Our loving heavenly Father, who had given His children every possible good and perfect gift, is betrayed. God showed humankind how much He cared, but man responded with heartless rejection. God had set one simple boundary for them to obey: "You are free to eat from any tree in the garden; but you must not eat from the tree of the knowledge of good and evil, for when you eat of it you will surely die" (Genesis 2:16).

The drama includes another character, the serpent, who tempted Adam and Eve into believing they would not die but that their eyes would be opened. The serpent preyed upon the emotional insecurity of Adam and Eve, and they succumbed to the ultimate temptation. We can sense God's disappointment.

Adam and Eve knew immediately that they had disobeyed and disappointed God. They were appropriately ashamed, and we see the development of more human emotion and a decision to hide from God. But God is God. He seeks out His disobedient children.

"The LORD God banished him from the Garden of Eden to work the ground from which he had been taken. After he drove the man out, he placed on the east side of the Garden of Eden cherubim and a flaming sword flashing back and forth to guard the way to the tree of life" (Genesis 3:23-24).

We have been created in the image of God, so we have the capacity to think, to reason, to decide, and to feel. We can imagine how God feels in this situation. He is emotional and relates to His children emotionally. He listens to Adam and Eve and understands them. Our emotions can move us in the direction intended for us. They are an incredibly powerful source of information, often enlightening us about critical decisions in our lives.

Edward Kaplan of Brandeis University, speaking about the famous Jewish theologian Abraham Joshua Heschel, stated, "Heschel's central idea…was a God of pathos, a God of emotions, a God who cares about human history and what human beings do, even individuals."[1]

Recently, I talked to a couple that had taken their two teenage children to Europe for a long-planned vacation. The parents had set aside money to stay in fancy hotels, allowing their children to order room service and eat at the nicest restaurants. For two weeks they pampered their children with the best gifts money could buy.

Upon their return I asked about their vacation, knowing they had high hopes that it would be a highlight of their family life.

The wife looked glumly at her husband. He looked squeamishly at me.

"Well," he began, "we were really disappointed."

Not hiding my surprise, I asked, "What happened? I thought this was going be the best vacation you'd ever had."

"Well," she said, "it seemed like the more we did for our kids, the more they wanted. They found something wrong with the hotels, they didn't like the European food, and they were even critical of the room service. We were so disappointed by their reaction. They acted like entitled brats most of the time. It was a very big letdown."

I wonder if God's heart was broken by Adam and Eve's behavior in much the same way. He had spared no expense to make the garden of Eden the finest accommodations possible. They had everything they could eat and all the beauty the world offered, and they were free to reign over all of creation. Still, it wasn't enough, and they blatantly disobeyed God.

God must have been profoundly disappointed with Adam and Eve. His heart must have sunk when He realized His children had disobeyed Him, even after all He had done for them. Was He saddened when He banished them from the garden? Did He weep when paradise was sullied with sin?

Old Testament Emotions

Adam and Eve were no longer perfect. Their lives weren't perfect, their relationship wasn't perfect, and their offspring wouldn't be perfect. History doesn't stop at the fall, however. In fact, the Old Testament is largely a narrative about the lives of His beloved nation of Israel—their obedience and disobedience and their emotion-packed stories. These are stories of God's personal involvement with His people, His ongoing delight in them, and His desire to make them prosperous (see Deuteronomy 30:9).

As we progress through the Old Testament, we read the accounts of humankind and see our lives in their lives. We see our emotions in their emotions. We see the ways they used their emotions effectively, making wise decisions, and ineffectively, allowing their emotions to play out in a destructive fashion.

Consider one of the first dramas to unfold outside the garden of Eden. Driven from paradise, Adam and Eve cobbled together a life by the sweat of their brows. We feel their loss and trauma as we ponder the cataclysmic event.

Adam and Eve wove together a life for a time. They had two children—Cain and Abel. The Scriptures tell us that Abel was a keeper of flocks while Cain worked the soil. They had learned the importance of making offerings to God, but Cain offered a feeble sacrifice.

"Cain brought some of the fruits of the soil as an offering to the LORD. But Abel brought fat portions from some of the firstborn of his flock. The LORD looked with favor on Abel and his offering, but on Cain and his offering he did not look with favor. So Cain was very angry, and his face was downcast" (Genesis 4:3-5).

Cain felt jilted. Although he made a poor attempt to please God, he was jealous that God was pleased with Abel's more thoughtful sacrifice.

The Lord noticed Cain's attitude and confronted him. "Why is your face downcast? If you do what is right, will you not be accepted? But if you do not do what is right, sin is crouching at your door; it desires to have you, but you must master it" (Genesis 4:6-7).

Cain faced a difficult decision, and like his parents, he failed the test. A few verses later we read of him killing his brother out of envy and spite.

Here we see destructive emotion run amok. We see in Cain what is in each of our hearts—the temptation to let emotion rule. We watch Cain react to his brother's favored position. We sense his burning anger turn to bitterness, hatred, and finally murder. His healthy emotions turned and twisted, destructively spiraling downward.

From this point on, we read the story of biblical characters—Noah, Abraham, Sarah, Isaac, Jacob, Joseph…people like you and me who interact with their world and with God largely by way of their emotions. Sometimes they listen wisely to their feelings, making sound decisions. Sometimes they let their emotions become unruly, making poor decisions.

The story of Noah and the flood is fascinating. Can you imagine the scene? God was sick of the wickedness on the earth and planned to destroy it and start anew. The plan to build an ark, however, couldn't have made a lot of sense to Noah. Surely naysayers were scoffing at him. Build a monstrous ark in an area of the world where little rain fell? Had people even seen rain (Genesis 2:4-7)? Can you imagine the derisive jeers from his neighbors? But God spoke to Noah's heart, and we read that Noah did everything God told him to do—and he and his family were spared.

In each biblical story, emotions and intellectual considerations are both included in decision making. In every circumstance, God allows His people to experience their emotions and to live with the consequences.

Laughter in the Bible

Biblical history is not all sadness. Ample doses of joy and celebration are woven through these stories. The story of Abram and Sarai has a particularly happy ending. During a time when having children was seen as a blessing from God, Sarai felt humiliation and disgrace at her barrenness. In that depressive state, she chose to give her maidservant to Abram to be his wife. However, when she found out Hagar was pregnant, she began to despise her as well as Abram.

"You are responsible for the wrong I am suffering. I put my servant in your arms, and now that she knows she is pregnant, she despises me. May the LORD judge between you and me" (Genesis 16:5). In her overwhelming bitterness, Sarai mistreats Hagar, and Hagar flees from her.

The story begins with Sarai feeling such intense jealousy, anger, and overwhelming bitterness that she becomes abusive to Hagar. Who could blame her? Every woman around her was having children, and this was seen as a blessing from God. She felt confused and rejected, wondering what she had done to be treated so harshly.

But God had not abandoned Sarai and Abram. Just when they believed they would be childless, God burst onto the scene in a big way. He told Abram that his name would be changed to Abraham, and Sarai would be Sarah. Although Abraham was 99 years old, God told him that his wife would bear him a son. Sarah laughed! It was too much to hope for, yet Abraham trusted God. After giving birth to Isaac, Sarah said, "God has brought me laughter, and everyone who hears about this will laugh with me" (Genesis 21:6). Joyful emotion filled their hearts.

Joy at the Prophecy of Jesus

The Old Testament story is filled with the fullness of humanity—complete with emotional twists and turns. We find drama, sadness, anger, excitement, discouragement, and delight. To read the Bible without attending to the emotional tones is to turn it into a dry, sterile document. The Scriptures have life—in large part because of the emotions involved in them. God is emotionally involved with His people.

The Old Testament is an emotion-packed narrative that builds like a symphonic crescendo to the coming of the Messiah. Listen to the voice of God, through His prophet Isaiah, tell about the coming of Jesus:

> Here is my servant, whom I uphold, my chosen one
> in whom I delight; I will put my Spirit on him and he will
> bring justice to the nations. He will not shout or cry out,
> or raise his voice in the streets. A bruised reed he will not
> break, and a smoldering wick he will not snuff out. In
> faithfulness he will bring forth justice; he will not falter or

be discouraged till he establishes justice on earth. In his law the islands will put their hope (Isaiah 42:1-4).

In perhaps one of the most poignant passages in Scripture, the prophet Isaiah foretells of Jesus' ministry:

> The Spirit of the Sovereign LORD is on me, because the LORD has anointed me to preach good news to the poor. He has sent me to bind up the brokenhearted, to proclaim freedom for the captives, and release from darkness for the prisoners, to proclaim the year of the LORD's favor and the day of vengeance of our God, to comfort all who mourn, and provide for those who grieve in Zion—to bestow on them a crown of beauty instead of ashes, the oil of gladness instead of mourning, and a garment of praise instead of a spirit of despair (Isaiah 61:1-3).

I love to read that passage when I feel as if everything is turning against me. Isaiah offers hopeful words to those who sink into the pit of discouragement. When our emotions overwhelm us, as they often do, he shares with us the heart of God—a heart of compassion, one that knows our struggles and relates to us as emotional people.

Emotions at Jesus' Arrival

The arrival of Jesus is riveting. In a land of political powermongers and religious zealots, even the highest and mightiest are frightened when they learn that a special infant has been born.

Word spread quickly that magi had visited from the east looking for this "king of the Jews." We might think someone as powerful as Herod would brush off rumors about a future king arriving as a baby. How could an infant, born in lowly Bethlehem, threaten his stronghold? But we read, "When King Herod heard this he was disturbed, and all Jerusalem with him. When he had called together all the people's chief priests and teachers of the law, he asked them where the Christ was to be born" (Matthew 2:3-4).

King Herod was frightened. He and the religious rulers knew about the prophecies concerning a Savior who would change history to save His people. Herod was aware of years of discord with the Jews and how the right man, at the right time, could catalyze a disturbance. He was threatened and frantically took immediate action to kill every child who could have possibly been this Savior.

But Herod's plot was foiled. God had other plans. He protected Mary and Joseph by sending them to Egypt to stay until Herod's death.

Jesus' Emotions

In the village of Bethlehem, a baby was born to a carpenter and young girl. Intrigue pervades the story as Mary becomes pregnant without having slept with any man.

What are you doing, God? Joseph must have asked. *What has she been doing? I've been made a fool. I'm not going to be a part of this. I'll divorce her quietly and get back to my old life as best as I can.*

But God touched Joseph's heart and told him that He had an astonishing plan for Joseph and Mary. He had chosen them to bring the Savior of the world into humanity.

To be told you would have a child without having slept together is incredible. To be told your son would be the Savior of humankind is unbelievable. An angel visits a teenage virgin and tells her she will give birth to the Messiah—this had to be a mysterious and frightening experience!

The biblical account says Mary was "greatly troubled" when the angel first spoke to her. She questioned how she, a virgin, could possibly be pregnant. The angel assured her that the Holy Spirit would come upon her, and she would give birth to the Son of God.

"I am the Lord's servant," Mary answered. "May it be to me as you have said." Here Mary sounds as if she is speaking from her head. She has yet to process what is happening to her, so she offers an obedient response.

Some time later Mary gave a more exuberant response from her heart—the Magnificat:

> My soul glorifies the Lord and my spirit rejoices in God my Savior, for he has been mindful of the humble state of his servant. From now on all generations will call me blessed, for the Mighty One has done great things for me—holy is his name (Luke 1:46-49).

Can you imagine Mary's emotions, now that she's had some time to understand what was happening to her? Joyful, perhaps even dancing, she now appears delighted in her future. She must have struggled to allow the power and immensity of this situation to settle in before determining how to approach the difficult days ahead.

Mary and Joseph were faithful—God had carefully chosen the people who would be intimately involved in bringing His one and only Son into the world to save people from sin. God's choice of Mary and Joseph was no mistake—it was ordered before the beginning of time.

The Gospels of Matthew, Mark, Luke, and John offer the accounts of the life of Jesus—told by those who walked and talked with Him. These are men whose lives were drastically altered by the carpenter's son from Nazareth. Luke's carefully researched account is secondhand (he was raised a Gentile), but the other three Gospel writers dined, danced, and even debated with Jesus. An honest and open-minded reading of their stories clearly reveals that Jesus was fully God and fully man. In fact, the apostle Paul shares this about Jesus:

> Who, being in very nature God, did not consider equality with God something to be grasped, but made himself nothing, taking the very nature of a servant, being made in human likeness. And being found in appearance as a man, he humbled himself and became obedient to death—even death on a cross" (Philippians 2:6-8).

What does this mean for us as we consider the relationship

between our emotions and our decision making? Consider these implications:

First, God chose to reveal Himself as a man. Let's face it—Jesus could have invaded the earth as the mighty warrior and king some had expected. He could have ridden onto the scene triumphant, declaring His reign and rule. But He didn't. He came to earth, God incarnate, as a humble human—fully God, fully man. Scripture tells us that because of His humanity, He can relate to us in all our weaknesses (Hebrews 4:15).

Second, being fully God and fully man, He felt every emotion we feel. He was familiar with temptation, struggle, grief, and joy. The Gospels offer us a glimpse into those times when He was disappointed with His disciples, angered by the money changers in the temple, and saddened at the death of His friend Lazarus. He questioned His heavenly Father at the time of His own death. Jesus was not a one-dimensional stick figure, but a complete, fully faceted man.

Third, Jesus didn't judge emotions as right or wrong but encouraged us to deal with them effectively and appropriately. Jesus didn't relegate emotions to the back of the decision-making bus. He listened intently to His disciples and friends and showed compassion for them. We never hear Him scolding them for their emotions—only for wrong actions.

A careful walk with Jesus through His many encounters with disciples and friends reveals His acceptance of one of the most fundamental aspects of our humanity—our emotions. He realized that connecting to people through their emotions is the way to make the most basic bonds. Such ties are created most often not through intellectual understanding but by way of the heart.

The Apostle Paul's Perspective

Jesus didn't come to earth as a conquering hero. He accepted the path of the suffering servant and gave people freedom to accept or reject Him. Many chose to scoff at the good news and many still find the gospel story too unbelievable to incorporate into their lives. Jesus allows them to choose. He promises, however, to return one day in triumph, as the apostle Paul says:

> Therefore God exalted him to the highest place and gave him the name that is above every name, that at the name of Jesus every knee should bow, in heaven and on earth and under the earth, and every tongue confess that Jesus Christ is Lord, to the glory of God the Father (Philippians 2:9-11).

Paul's story is an improbable one. Formerly known as Saul, he was a fervent persecutor of Christians and the church. He never walked with Jesus before the crucifixion, as did most of the apostles. Saul was a Roman citizen and Jew who hated Christians until his encounter with Jesus. Saul was knocked down on the Damascus Road. Blinded by a light brighter than the sun, he heard the voice of Jesus: "Saul, Saul, why do you persecute me?" (Acts 9:4).

Saul was instructed to go into the city and meet with Ananias. For three days he was blind and did not eat or drink anything. Several days later in Damascus, Ananias laid his hands on him and healed him. From then on, Saul spent time with the disciples and began preaching the gospel.

The book of Acts and Paul's letters provide a fascinating view of his humanity. He despised and resented Christians and actively participated in their deaths, but then he had a conversion experience of monstrous proportions. His life was dramatically changed, and he devoted his life to preaching the gospel and planting churches. His anger turned to love. His resentment turned to dedication to the cause of Christ. In the process we see a full picture of his humanity—both his intellectual prowess and his emotional energy.

Once the "worst of sinners" (1 Timothy 1:16), Paul allows the living Christ to invade his heart and change him. After Paul's conversion, we see him give any credit due him to the Lord. He repeatedly declares that he is not worthy to be called an apostle because of his earlier behavior. He cannot seem to gain mastery over his emotions and behavior: "I do not understand what I do. For what I want to do I do not do, but what I hate I do" (Romans 7:15). Yet just a few verses later he encourages us in our struggle with the same passions, emotions, and behaviors: "Therefore, there is now no condemnation for those who are in Christ Jesus, because through Christ Jesus the law of the Spirit of life set me free from the law of sin and death" (Romans 8:1)

Hope is available for you and me. Paul wrestled with unruly emotions and behaviors. He suffered the angst of not knowing why he still had a thorn in his flesh (2 Corinthians 12:7) that he prayed would be removed. He did things he didn't want to do and didn't do the things he wanted to do.

Sounds a lot like me.

Stories Penned by Men

As we read Old and New Testament stories, we repeatedly sense the emotional heart of God. Every story in the Bible is penned by a man but inspired by the Holy Spirit. "All Scripture is God-breathed and is useful for teaching, rebuking, correcting and training in righteousness, so that the man of God may be thoroughly equipped for every good work" (2 Timothy 3:16). God used men and their distinctive personalities, emotional bents, and individual writing styles to pen the Word of God.

As we read the biblical stories of men and women, we are moved by their emotional dramas. We are inspired by the story of Ruth and her kinsman-redeemer, Boaz, or of Queen Esther and her narrow escape from death, or of Nehemiah rebuilding the wall around Jerusalem, or of Moses leading Israel out of Egypt, or of King David's rise and fall from power. But more importantly, we see the heart of God in these stories.

Ruth's story is my story. David, the youngest son of Jesse (as well as Ruth's grandson, and in the lineage of Joseph, father of Jesus), was chosen as heir to the throne because of his tender and loving heart, and that gives me hope that God sees my heart as well. Their vulnerability is my vulnerability. Their emotional struggles are my emotional struggles, and their triumphs, my triumphs.

Body, Mind, and Spirit

Reading through Scripture, we clearly see that we are more than a mass of fiber, muscles, and tissue. Paul repeatedly focuses our attention on our minds and encourages us to set our minds on what the Spirit desires (Romans 8:5-6) and on things above (Colossians 3:2). He explains that we can be renewed in the spirit of our minds (Ephesians 4:23) and transformed by the renewing of our minds (Romans 12:1).

But Paul never advocated a merely ethereal spirituality. He also stressed paying attention to our bodies. "Your body is a temple of the Holy Spirit...therefore honor God with your body" (1 Corinthians 6:19-20).

Scripture also states we have been created in the likeness of God, and that likeness includes a spiritual nature, which includes our emotions. Some people would say our emotions are part of our body, but I believe they are part of our spiritual nature. Either way, we cannot deny that we are emotional creatures. We react to events not only from a mental perspective but also by the way they make us feel.

Some people believe that when Scripture refers to our heart, it includes our emotions. The psalmist cries out to God, "who searches minds and hearts" (Psalm 7:9). The writer to the Hebrews says, "For the word of God is living and active. Sharper than any double-edged sword, it penetrates even to dividing soul and spirit, joints and marrow; it judges the thoughts and attitudes of the heart" (Hebrews 4:12).

Clearly, we are part physical and part spiritual. We have thoughts and intentions of the heart as well as a spiritual nature that includes emotions. Any attempt to divide us generates immense challenges—we were created as unified persons, and our emotions are a powerful aspect of that nature.

Respecting Our Emotions

We certainly do not want to place our emotions on the throne of life. Although I sometimes feel as if mine have mounted an insurrection and are ruling the day, that is not what God desires. Everything, including our intellect, will, and emotions, is to come under the authority of Scripture and of God.

So we do not bow to our emotions, but we do respect them. To ignore our emotions, as many people do, is to invite trouble. Many doctors agree that emotional challenges cause at least half of all patient visits. Lots of physical maladies have emotional components, and professionals have embraced the process of healing emotions as a path to healing physical problems. Our emotions are a vital aspect of our nature, an integral part that warrants respect.

As a clinical psychologist, I cannot imagine working with people and their problems without listening to their emotions. How they feel about something or someone is a vital aspect of how they relate to that situation or person. I must understand their emotions if I am to honestly attend to their situation. If I am to promote healing on the inside and on the outside, I must accurately and honestly attend to their emotional life.

The Bible tells us that the issues of life flow from the heart (Proverbs 4:23 NKJV). The word *heart* refers to our soul—usually considered to be our mind, will, and emotions. Each part affects the other. Changing the way we think often changes how we feel. Turning our will over to the power of Christ in our lives will undoubtedly affect our emotions. Understanding our emotions and dealing with them in an honest and compassionate way will help us physically and spiritually.

Inviting God In

Consider the possibility that God speaks to you through your emotional life. This may be a challenge because emotions have been suspect at best. I remember learning in Sunday school that the locomotive to the spiritual life was faith, followed by facts, with the caboose being feelings. I learned to devalue my emotions.

Actually, emotions provide the perfect opportunity to connect with God. Like the psalmist who, in his turmoil, cried out to God, we too have an opportunity in our difficulties not only to invite God in but also to listen more closely to His voice.

Our times of weakness and confusion are perfect opportunities to seek clarity from God. In these special places where we bring our emotions to God, we can see things from His perspective. We can listen to what He wants to say to us in our fragile moments. We can learn about areas of sin that need special attention.

The challenge, of course, is to be tuned in to our emotions so we can invite God in. If we wall off our emotions, as we often do, we separate parts of ourselves from His powerful influence. If, on the other hand, we walk gently with our emotions, we have an opportunity to open ourselves to God so He can help us heal and lead us in new paths. God gives us new strength, new vision, and new avenues for dealing with our emotional lives.

Our prayer, as we move together through this book, must be the same as that of the apostle Paul in his letter to the Thessalonians: "May God himself, the God of peace, sanctify you through and through. May your whole spirit, soul and body be kept blameless at the coming of our Lord Jesus Christ. The one who calls you is faithful and he will do it" (1 Thessalonians 5:23).

I invite you to join me as we learn more about how to name and embrace our emotions—anticipating that we will hear the voice of God in the process.

2

Naming and Embracing
Our Emotions

*Recognizing the shutdown of feelings is
how emotional presence begins.*

RAPHAEL CUSHNIR

For many years I lived in a waterfront home near Hammersley Inlet, a spiny, seven-mile waterway jutting out of the south end of Puget Sound. Hammersley flows almost directly east to west, as narrow as 150 feet across in some places, and is known for its dramatic tidal action. Changes between high and low tide can be as much as 16 feet, with the water flowing at five miles per hour.

Puget Sound has long been a wonderful place to live because of the temperate climate and outdoor possibilities, many having to do with life on the water. It is a kayaker's paradise. Countless inlets, islands, and secret coves are waiting to be explored, albeit carefully because of the tides and weather.

Kayaking looks easy, and it can be if the kayaker has respect for the elements. Caution is the key in these churning waters. What you see on the surface is not always the same as what is taking place below.

Emotions are like tidal currents—an underlying force to be understood and respected. The kayaker who ignores the power of the

Hammersley current may end up in trouble. Those who disregard the slack water may end up in a roiling, rising tide, tossed around like a matchstick. This can also be true of anyone who ignores the power of emotions.

Like the tide that effortlessly bears the kayaker along, our emotions can carry us. They can either toss us about and make us feel out of control, or they can motivate us to take effective action. In this chapter, we'll highlight the power of emotions and learn to understand them and use them for effective action.

Emotional Decision Making

Emotional decision making is the process of listening to our emotions and using them as an influential guide to making healthy choices about our lives. It is the process of being mindful of our emotions, considering what they tell us and using that information to help us make wise decisions.

Notice that I said that emotional decision making is a process. There is no simple recipe for listening to our feelings and then making a snap judgment based on them. Most people have lived a long time relegating their feelings to the last place in line behind the faith and facts they learned about at church and school. Uncomfortable with these powerful, unseen forces, they are tempted to stifle them. In fact, many people are so uncomfortable and frightened of this emotional energy—energy in motion—that they are unable to name it, let alone utilize it.

The first step in harnessing and utilizing this profound energy for decision making is to name it. Discerning the emotions you feel and defining exactly what they tell you require effort and skill.

Notice also that I emphasize listening to your feelings. Just as kayakers are in tune with the currents and tides, emotional decision makers are tuned to their feelings. They've developed an understanding of these feelings and discerned what they indicate. By reading this book and applying what you learn, you can develop a much better awareness of your emotions. You can also become sensitive to your feelings without allowing them to drive you. The astute emotional decision maker strives for balance.

Furthermore, you will see that emotions can be an influential guide. We will not bow down to emotions as if they were the final authority in our lives. Emotions are influential, and we should always consider them wisely. The emotion of fear, for example, must be considered thoughtfully. Just because we are afraid of something does not mean we should not do it. Sometimes fear is a flashing yellow light warning us of danger, but at other times it is False Evidence Appearing as Real (FEAR.)

Finally, we will learn to use emotions to help us make healthy choices about our lives. After all, our emotions, like the tidal current, can propel us toward our goals or spin us around like a boxer bouncing off the ropes to absorb another blow. Our goal is to harness the power of our emotions and become wise, thoughtful, and emotional decision makers.

E-Motions

The avid kayaker heads out into open waters thoroughly prepared, having studied the winds and tides and knowing what to expect. Optimum conditions work together to move the craft briskly about without capsizing it or pushing it off course. The kayaker skims along in harmony with the tide and winds as the sun casts a long light over the water. Being accurately tuned in to our emotional energy can be just as exhilarating.

Yet I've been on the water under the exact opposite conditions—fighting the tide, struggling against the wind, nervously scanning a dark and threatening sky. These conditions make for a long afternoon. The key is to have respect for each of these influences and to understand their power.

We have seen that emotions are energy in motion. They are filled with energy that we can use either constructively or destructively.

A woman wrote a note to me recently, describing the despair she was experiencing.

"I am married to a man who has a pornography addiction. He is a leader in the church and has asked me to be careful choosing whom I talk with about this problem. I have caught him looking at this filth on the Internet many times, and each time he tells me he is sorry and won't do it again. He is such a good man, and I love him, but am not sure what to do about this problem. I am angry, frightened, confused, discouraged, and uncertain about how to proceed. Please help."

You sense this woman's profound struggle. You can hear and feel her emotional angst. She is hard-pressed to define exactly what she is feeling, citing emotions such as anger, confusion, and despair. She is feeling a tidal current of emotion.

We can also sense that she is not experiencing a free flow of energy in motion, another common problem we will address in this book. She is stuck in her confusion. Rather than letting her anger lead to decisive action, she allows it to become stifled, commingled with other feelings. She allows herself to become overwhelmed with discouragement, leading to inaction.

Many people struggle to allow their emotions to flow smoothly and freely, a problem apparent in this case. The energy in motion seems to be dammed up inside her as she struggles to express it. Naming and embracing her energy in motion will help her make healthy choices in her life.

Dammed-Up Emotions

In a perfect world, we embrace and listen to clearly defined emotions and then allow them to influence us as we make healthy choices. However, this perfect world doesn't exist, and many of us struggle to name our emotions, embrace them, and allow them to point us toward healthy decisions.

The woman who wrote the note faces a significant problem.

The husband she loves and admires is caught in the throes of addiction—an all-too-common ailment. Her response, however, offers us additional clues to her emotions and her problem.

First, her husband relapses repeatedly into his pornography addiction, leading to greater emotional upheaval. This is not a one-time occurrence, so we shouldn't be surprised that this woman is discouraged. We can imagine that she has confronted him, prayed with him, and loved him, all without seeing any significant change.

Second, she might be enabling his addiction to continue, thus exacerbating her emotional turmoil. When we solve problems and deal with them effectively, our emotional life follows suit. We are encouraged to see positive results and discouraged when the problem recurs. Her discouragement could be a powerful impetus for change.

Third, notice the progression of her energy in motion. She says she is angry, confused, discouraged, and despairing. Her various feelings offer a clue as to how her emotional life can be of assistance to her. Perhaps reading her story evokes feelings of empathy for her, or perhaps you feel anger that she is living with a man who professes the Christian faith but lives a double standard.

As I note the progression of her energy in motion, I wonder if she stops herself from embracing her anger and discouragement. Were she to name and embrace her anger, she might take more decisive action with her husband by setting firmer limits. She might find that her anger turns into righteous indignation and leads to swift action. This was the case with Jesus in the temple.

Fourth, she seems to settle into feelings of uncertainty and confusion. Many people who avoid emotional decision making get mired in uncertainty. Perhaps she is afraid of her stronger feelings; perhaps she fears taking action. Confusion may be a safer place, but she is stuck.

Finally, emotions denied are intensified. Despair and depression, as we'll learn later in this book, are often the result of anger denied.

Many Christians are uncomfortable with these powerful emotions and are more comfortable with softer emotions such as discouragement and despair. Dammed-up emotions, however, often lead to trouble. They compound the problem rather than solve it.

I encouraged this woman to pay close attention to her feelings, listening to what each was telling her. I encouraged her to pay close attention to the natural flow of her feelings, considering what appropriate action she could take. She ultimately decided to set healthy boundaries with her husband, tolerating less and seeking intervention for his problems.

Paying Attention

Why are feelings intensified when we deny them? Like holding a balloon under water, we may continue suppressing our emotions, expending valuable energy. However, the balloon may slip out of our grasp and shoot to the surface chaotically and uncontrolled, throwing us out of balance. Or instead, we may slowly and skillfully allow the emotions to rise in a manner that allows us to carefully examine and address them.

Raphael Cushnir, author of *Setting Your Heart on Fire,* shares some important insights about this process of attending to our emotions. "In order to open to your feelings, you need to pay attention to them. Paying attention to what you're feeling is a simple act. It's simple, but not easy. To pay attention consistently requires breaking habits that may have developed over decades."[1]

This sounds like such simple counsel: To accomplish this goal, we must pay attention to our feelings. But as Cushnir rightly adds, we must break habits learned over decades. Let's consider some of the barriers that keep us from listening to our feelings. Then let's consider new skills for naming them.

First, we've been trained to stifle our emotions. This is a profound and debilitating barrier to our work. I've never taken a class in discerning and labeling my emotions. The only instruction I received, prior to graduate work in psychology, was what *not* to feel and what not to do. I can still hear my parents' strict injunctions about certain feelings:

"Don't cry. Be tough and get back out on the field."

"Don't be mad at your sisters. They're smaller than you, and you're the older brother."

"Stop whining."

"Cheer up. Lots of other kids would love to have the problems you have."

"There's nothing to be afraid of. Be strong and get going."

Second, we've never been trained to name our emotions. I can't remember a time when my parents helped me name my feelings, though they were always loving and kind. No one helped me differentiate anger from hurt, sadness from discouragement, fear from apprehension. I doubt that my parents possessed these skills, so they couldn't have helped me in this process. Otherwise, they might have offered helpful comments like these:

"You sound hurt that Donald didn't invite you to spend the evening with him."

"I can hear that you're sad about not making the basketball team. It never feels good to miss out on something you hoped for."

"You sound very angry at your sisters. Let's talk about how you can express that anger effectively."

Third, we've never been encouraged to embrace our emotions. For so long, people have considered emotions a nuisance, something that got in the way of something more important. If a friend hurt you by rejecting you, others probably taught you to simply ignore those feelings and let the situation roll off your back. If you were angry at a sibling or friend, you were probably told to get over it.

Finally, we've never been taught the usefulness of feelings. Feelings are *not* extraneous things that get in the way of daily functioning. They can actually provide useful energy in our decision-making process. In fact, they are essential to making healthy decisions. This way of thinking may be new and very foreign to you. Indeed, we have a lot of unlearning to do!

Cushnir goes on to offer this advice in naming and embracing the process: "Remember, paying attention to feelings is not the same as expressing, exaggerating, or acting out. All it requires is a gentle focus, a turning inward toward what's already present."[2]

Take a moment to attend to what you are feeling. Listen to your body and its sensations as well as the mood you are in. Picture a list of emotions and search for the one that might fit your state. Check the following list and finish this sentence: Right now I feel…

Happy	Angry	Excited	Frustrated
Anxious	Discouraged	Proud	Curious
Hopeful	Lonely	Calm	Sad

Were you able to attach yourself to any of these feelings? Did more than one seem to fit your situation? No one said you are allowed to feel only one emotion at a time. In fact, we often feel confused and ambivalent before we can actually name our feelings.

Misunderstanding and Maligning Emotions

I commonly work with individuals who dismiss emotions. I am surprised, however, at how often people who struggle with "emotional problems" are reluctant to explore the very emotions that are causing them so much pain.

Kerry came to see me recently for symptoms of depression. This 40-year-old man had never married but had been involved with a woman for the past few years.

Burly but neatly dressed with a matter-of-fact disposition, Kerry couldn't understand why he was struggling with depression.

"I'm a chemical engineer at Weyerhaeuser," he told me. "I have a great job, and I'm doing well financially. It's ridiculous that I would feel depressed. A lot of people are a lot worse off than I am."

Kerry appeared sullen as he shared with me. He moved slowly, spoke haltingly, and lacked ambition and energy to change his circumstances.

"Depression is usually a mixture of many different feelings," I said, "and we need to explore what's going on under the surface."

"Sounds like a waste of time to me," he countered. "I don't plan on spending a year in therapy."

"That's fine," I said. "But if we're going to understand why you're depressed, we have to determine what might be feeding that depression."

"I've read about depression, and much of it seems to be biochemical. I don't know if I really believe that depression comes from emotional problems."

"Depression can certainly have a biochemical aspect," I said. "I'm not saying that you have emotional problems. But that's the first place to look when someone has symptoms of depression or anxiety or other problems. Why don't we just talk about your life and let me listen objectively? How does that sound?"

"Okay. What do you want to know?"

"Let's start with your work and your relationship with your girlfriend."

The more Kerry shared, the more discouraged he became. He had worked in the papermaking industry for 25 years, and though he made an excellent wage, he didn't enjoy his job. He had always wanted to be an architect or designer but had jumped at this position out of college and never left. He felt imprisoned by golden handcuffs. The money was simply too good to leave.

Kerry was clearly angry with himself for staying with the job but had suppressed his anger, except for occasional jabs he'd take at the company and his "redneck" colleagues. He struggled to identify his feelings and seemed reluctant to consider that his emotional life could affect his physical well-being.

He went on to talk about his girlfriend in much the same way. He told me that he didn't love her but that she loved him and appreciated him.

"How can I leave her when she tells me I'm her life? She's wrapped herself around me, and I don't feel right about walking away."

"Do you want to stay with her, Kerry?" I asked. "Are you happy with her?"

"I'm not really *un*happy. I've never found a woman who totally excited me. I'm not sure I believe in soul mates, so maybe this is as good as it gets."

"Tell me how you feel when you're with her," I said.

"It's okay. Not really good or bad. Not happy or sad. I'm not sure I'm doing her any favors by staying with her. I don't really love her and don't want to spend the rest of my life with her. I'm kind of numb, I guess."

"It sounds like you've settled," I said. "You're ignoring your unhappiness and trying to tell yourself that things are okay when they're not."

Kerry was typical of the many people who push feelings away and tell themselves that they can't trust their emotions. Although he knew he was not happy, facing that truth during that first session was too risky for him. That would become the focus of our work together in subsequent sessions.

Society Says

Much of my work encouraging people to name and embrace their emotions feels like kayaking in the currents of Hammersley Inlet. We sense the underlying energy and tension of emotions and feel them tossing us around, but taking the time to name and embrace them is another matter. To make matters worse, society works against us. Pia Melody, author of *Facing Codependence,* elaborates:

> Our culture divides our feelings into two kinds: "good" and "bad." Anger, pain, fear, guilt, and shame are labeled bad or negative. Joy we consider good or positive. Unfortunately, this sort of "black or white" categorizing is erroneous and dysfunctional.[3]

Certainly we can relate to what Melody is saying. We send children the message that they should be rational and in control of their emotions. We teach them to stay away from "bad" feelings—and they learn very quickly which ones are bad: anger, fear, sadness, resentment, and unhappiness.

Melody explains how our culture teaches men not to express fear. If men are afraid, they are cowards. Conversely, women are allowed to be frightened because they are supposed to be weak and vulnerable. Meanwhile, men are supposed to protect women from everything that is threatening.

Society allows men to be angry. That is a male privilege, even though this anger has wreaked havoc on our culture since the beginning of time. Women are not supposed to be angry, and when they are angry, they're "aggressive." Men are particularly uncomfortable with women who are powerful or who appear angry.

Acknowledging pain is unacceptable for either sex. The message from society is that if we're in pain, we must do whatever is necessary to numb it. We have little tolerance for suffering, regardless of how legitimate.

These cultural messages caused Kerry a great deal of confusion, which we worked on in counseling. He had to learn to tell himself the truth. His emotions were not good or bad, but they were extremely useful in determining what he needed to change in his life.

Embracing Our Emotions

I encouraged Kerry to begin journaling—a practice I routinely recommend to people who want to understand their emotional lives. I encouraged him to make an entry every day, noting what he felt, thought, and wanted. I encouraged him to note a particular emotion, such as sadness, happiness, joy, anger, frustration, or one of the hundreds of others he might be experiencing at that time.

Why do I recommend this practice? I'm completely convinced that our emotions contain vital information for successfully conducting our lives. I'm convinced that we intuitively know a whole lot more than we want to admit.

Kerry proved my theory—he soon discovered that he was angry about being trapped in a dead-end relationship. Although he was uncertain about the validity of the dream of having a soul mate who shared his goals, dreams, and passions, he hoped it might be true. He discovered that he was very frustrated with his girlfriend. He didn't like many of her attributes and felt they were ill-suited for one another. They didn't share many of the same goals, values, or dreams. As I suspected, he felt like he was settling, which led to his feeling trapped and depressed.

Kerry didn't come to these realizations quickly. More than once he cancelled appointments, ostensibly because of work obligations. When he did attend, we discussed the possibility that he didn't truly believe in embracing emotions. Initially, he refused to consider the possibility that his emotions could lead him in a better direction. He gradually discovered, however, that he was frightened about the possibility of altering his safe and comfortable but depressing lifestyle.

Consider again the possibility of embracing your emotions. Begin by journaling every day what you feel, think, and want. Consider inviting God into that process, asking what He may want for your life. What are your passions? What do you want to accomplish? What excites you? The answers can move you in the right direction.

An Emotional Shake-Up

Embracing emotions can be frightening because it often leads us to shake up the status quo. Emotional energy takes us from one place to another. Our emotions move us. That's why they are energy in motion.

Some people have said that "there can be no breakthrough without a breakdown." This certainly applies to our emotional lives. For effective change to occur, we need to listen to our emotions, evaluate them, and make decisions accordingly. Our emotions are often accurate indicators that something needs to change. Restlessness, anxiety, or feelings of discouragement are signals that our lives must undergo some type of transformation.

Kerry became increasingly agitated as he discovered his unhappiness and realized that he wanted more from his life. I saw this as a good sign—he was becoming increasingly dissatisfied with his old life. Emotionally, he was ready to shake up things.

As Kerry became aware of his dissatisfaction with his work and relationship, he also became anxious about where this path might lead. If he didn't like his work as much as he thought, was he willing to start over with something new? If he was unhappy with his girlfriend after investing much of the past two years into that relationship, was he ready to endure a period of loneliness and begin searching for someone new? He would almost certainly endure a time of loss, which he had long been avoiding.

Kerry didn't like the emotional shake-up that occurred in counseling. He had grown accustomed to fitting his emotions into a neat little box. His emotions were in a rut, but the rut felt comfortable and familiar to him. Tipping the box of emotions upside down caused uncertainty and discomfort.

Learning to name and embrace emotions is a tricky process. We need to anticipate that the process will bring change and some unrest. If we can label this transition as normal, and even healthy, we will fare better. If we can anticipate crossing an uncomfortable emotional bridge before our feelings settle down on the other side, we'll cope more effectively with this time of uncertainty.

Emotional Wholeness

Emotional unrest is a precursor to positive change and wholeness. Tending to your various feelings, regardless of how uncomfortable the journey becomes, is the first step in a healthy new direction.

Many people raise their eyebrows when I give them the assignment of journaling about their thoughts and feelings. They are unfamiliar with journaling and equally unfamiliar with listening to their emotions. We are accustomed to tuning in to what others think we ought to feel or ways we ought to behave, so we have a hard time discerning our own true voices. We have stopped listening to our inner voices and the voice of God and have become strangers to them.

No wonder many of us walk around feeling fragmented, confused, and uncertain about what we think and feel. We *are* fragmented. We *have* dissociated ourselves from many of our painful feelings and uncomfortable thoughts. Emotional decision making is about reintegration. It is about reclaiming lost parts of ourselves and using those parts—our hidden thoughts and feelings—to make better decisions about our lives.

To achieve emotional wholeness and make healthy emotional decisions, we must decipher which voices are ours and which ones come from outside us. Learning to distinguish strong and powerful voices (such as our parents') from our own can be a huge challenge. What if our feelings run contrary to what society, our parents, our church, or our friends think we should feel and think? (The word *should* is a red flag. Trying to determine what we *should* feel is almost never helpful.)

Kerry's debilitating depression helped him see that he didn't understand parts of himself. Though deeply spiritual, he never considered that God might use his emotional life as a way to guide him. He never considered that his emotions might contain valuable information to lead him into a more fully functioning life.

Let's reflect on the feelings Kerry discovered and the ways they were helpful to him.

Kerry learned that he was lonely for a companion who shared his love of art, adventure, and travel. His girlfriend didn't share those interests, and subsequently he had abandoned his interest in them. He wanted a companion to share those interests with him, and he wanted to regain that part of himself as well. He had lost some integral, vital aspects of his personality that he now hoped to recover.

Kerry was discouraged and unhappy with his job. He recognized that his work was no longer a good fit for him. Although it paid well and had given him an opportunity to make financial gains, it didn't give him the creative opportunities he needed. The job didn't help him express his true passions; it actually stifled those expressions.

Kerry was frightened about the prospect of making changes. What would he do about his job, which he had held for most of his adult life? He was concerned about whether he could salvage it while being true to the new aspects of his personality he was uncovering. What would he do about his girlfriend, with whom he no longer felt compatible? He felt close to her, however, and a sense of compassion for her. How would he end that relationship? How would he feel when he was alone?

Kerry also felt encouraged, knowing that he was being called to live a more authentic life. He wanted to feel whole, and he knew he needed to make some decisions in order to be true to himself and to the voice of God in his life.

This is an exciting and frightening time for Kerry. He is still with his girlfriend and wonders if and how he might break free from this codependency. He doubts his own voice, his unique feelings. He is unsteady on his emotional feet, and that is to be expected. I encourage him to take one small step at a time. I encourage him to pay special attention to what God might be saying to him in the midst of his personal crisis.

God's Small Voice

"Be still, and know that I am God" (Psalm 46:10).

This passage is often quoted when we are being instructed about how to listen for the voice of God. I agree with that counsel. However, we can hear the voice of God in other ways too, and one way is to pay attention to our emotions.

As I write these words I am looking out on the snowcapped peaks of the Olympic Mountains. Few places in the world touch my heart and spirit as deeply as these jagged mountains.

What do I feel when I witness this grandeur? The psalmist wrote emotionally about the majesty of God's creation: "When I consider the heavens, the work of your fingers, the moon and the stars, which you have set in place, what is man that you are mindful of him, the son of man that you care for him?" (Psalm 8:3-4).

But what do I feel when I gaze out at these rugged mountains, their reflections shimmering across the expanse of Hood Canal? I feel awe, peacefulness, and excitement. These images stir something within me. I feel blessed and content. I feel connected to my Creator. I hear a small voice say to me, *David, I've created you to enjoy My creation. I've created you to love water, mountains, and rugged majesty. These are My gifts to you.*

I must be quiet in order to enjoy these gifts. If I am too caught up in deadlines, agendas, and intentions, I miss His gifts. If I have too much other clutter in my mind, I cannot meditate or consider His majesty.

I have many other emotions besides awe and contentment, to be sure. Just last evening I asked my wife, Christie, to sit with me and listen to the rumblings of my heart. Anger and resentment percolated in me. I needed to talk to someone, and she listened.

Before I could share my feelings with Christie, I asked myself if I would be safe sharing these emotions. I even asked if sharing them was the right thing to do. A small voice was accusing me that I should (red flag!) be over these past hurts, but I wasn't.

I was still wounded and resentful about events I had endured. I was angry about having been mugged in a park by a group of drunken Marines when I was a young man. Tears welled up inside me from places I hadn't touched in a while. Christie listened gently, and I felt a step closer to healing.

Even in the midst of these gurgling emotions, I sensed God inviting me to attend to them. They needed a voice. I sensed God had something to say to me about unfinished business in my life.

Mary Cartledgehayes, in her wonderful book *Grace: A Memoir,* talks of her time in seminary. She tells us how she and her colleagues recognized a temptation even in the church to deny feelings, as if God couldn't handle some of our more troubling emotions. In a small group discussion, one of her colleagues shared her thoughts: "None of the church liturgies ever address [anger]. They're sterile in that they don't touch deep feelings. Everything we do and say seems intentionally benign, as though God can't take our anger or disappointment."

Cartledgehayes adds, "Maybe we'd discovered the reason many of our colleagues seemed flat emotionally. If you think God can't contend with anger or disappointment, and consequently close off those feelings in yourself, you're bound to have to close off other feelings as well."[4]

I wonder, as Cartledgehayes suggests, if we unwittingly continue this incredible conspiracy to sterilize our relationship with God. I wonder if we try to keep our relationship with God one-dimensional, absent the gritty, ragged emotions many of us keep locked inside.

If it is true that emotions aren't right or wrong, and if God actually cares about all of me, then He cares about all my feelings. He cares about my unfinished anger and hurt and disappointment and resentment. As I am able to sit with those uncomfortable feelings, He will sit with me and help me address them. He promises to care for me and guide me into paths of healing. But before that can happen, I must be willing to attend to those feelings and listen to His small voice in the midst of them.

Now that we've considered the importance of naming and embracing our emotions, in the next chapter we'll explore exactly how these feelings can help us or hinder us in hearing God's voice.

3

Emotions:
Pathway to God

*The amazing thing is it's not that easy to stifle
awareness. It requires constant diligence. You have to
really work at it to be miserable.*

Paul Williams

My wife and I have been church shopping. We moved to a new
city and said goodbye to the congregation we had been a part of for
the previous two years. We left an Evangelical Covenant church, the
same denomination and worship format in which I was raised.

If you've ever church shopped, you know it can be a trying but
sometimes humorous experience. One church plied us with promises
of coffee, donuts, and eternal life. Enticed by all three, we decided to
give the place a try. But minutes after entering the school cafeteria
that served as a makeshift sanctuary, I wanted to leave.

The band began rocking with gospel songs as we searched for
folding chairs. People jumped up and down, waving their arms and
belting out the songs. I nervously eyed the door.

"The band is too loud!" I yelled into my wife's ear.

"C'mon," she said, "let's give it a chance."

Minutes later, the band was still banging out songs I didn't know, and I was feeling increasingly uncomfortable. I insisted we leave.

Not one to make a scene, my wife tried to dissuade me.

"I'm not changing my mind," I said. I knew this was not the right fit for me. With that we slipped out the door.

Shaken but undaunted, we vowed to try something a little different the following week. The next church was just the opposite of the previous one. It was the church my wife had attended 30 years earlier.

People who recognized Christie greeted her warmly. The average age of the congregation was 72, and the bulletins were printed on the same made-to-order sheets that my church used when I was a boy. An elderly organist played the three hymns, and a thin, short pastor read the notes of his sermon in a strained voice. I was dying for the entire 75 minutes. Once again I tried to talk Christie into leaving, but she put her foot down this time.

Our next outing was to a megachurch in a nearby town. The main level and balcony there provided plenty of room for us to go unnoticed if we needed to make a hasty getaway. But this church had possibilities. With a contemporary pianist, a lively choir, and a dynamic pastor who used PowerPoint presentations, we were tempted by the possibilities. The bulletin listed three pages of activities—something for every age and personality. But we eventually felt lost in the sea of people, the preaching a bit too "high gloss," and the worship style was still not quite right.

Not yet feeling that we had found "the one," last Sunday we went to church in a movie theater. The fit was just right. The preaching was solid, the singing not too long or too loud, and the people were friendly. We'll give it another chance.

Churches are a bit like emotions—some feel good, some don't. Some feel welcoming, some don't. Some have mixtures of good and bad in them, just like emotions. Some are unsettling, while others make you feel good all over.

Other similarities come to mind. Just as some people feel more comfortable with certain emotions, each of these churches had members who felt comfortable with certain types of worship experiences. Just as there are no right or wrong churches—provided that they are Bible-based—there are no right or wrong emotions.

A Variety of Emotions

We often feel more comfortable with certain emotions and distinctly less comfortable with others.

Unlike a lot of men, I'm more comfortable with feelings of happiness and sadness. I definitely don't like anger, and I am afraid of fear.

I can trace much of my emotional development to my family life. My father made a huge impression on me. He made it clear that we were not to display anger toward our siblings, of which I have four. Getting along well with one another was tantamount to being a good human being. I rarely saw my dad angry, but when he was, the entire family shuddered.

Thankfully, my family was comfortable with happiness and joy. My parents and siblings were able to express positive feelings openly. I took this for granted then, but I appreciate it now because I realize that many families don't enjoy the happiness I had as a child. Many people are simply unable to openly express happiness, as if by doing so they violate some unspoken family code of sobriety.

As I've said, learning to identify and name our feelings is no small task, especially since we've been trained to identify only a small portion of our feelings and then to label them as either good or bad. The bad ones, of course, we avoid and even deny. Like the churches that made me uncomfortable, we learn to dodge them and thus never fully appreciate them. A full range of feelings remains outside our awareness.

Giving Up Labels

Before we can determine whether an emotion is helpful and useful in our decision making, we must let go of the idea that certain emotions are good and others are bad. I learned that anger was bad, so I have never fully appreciated how it can be a valuable emotion. Likewise, my fear of fear can be paralyzing rather than useful.

Let's quit labeling emotions as good or bad. All emotions can teach us something and help us in our decision-making process. God gave us every emotion, and we can use each one as a means of communicating with Him. When we accept our emotions, we open myriad possibilities in our lives.

Consider again the challenges we create when we label our emotions as either good or bad.

Sandy is a bright 35-year-old woman who came to see me for counseling after the dissolution of her 15-year marriage. Thin, pinched-faced, and professional, Sandy has a tendency toward depression, stemming from years of oppressive control by her ex-husband.

Sandy became extremely codependent in her marriage, always working to meet her husband's every need. But regardless of what she did to please him, he was unhappy. Whenever she tried to encourage him to see the bright side of their lives, he found something to complain about. Consequently, Sandy began to view life as discouraging as well.

Sandy spent so many years tuned in to her ex's needs and feelings that she neglected her own. In fact, much of the time, she didn't know what she was feeling—she only knew that whatever she felt must be wrong because she was never able to please her husband.

"I learned to feel helpless with him," she said. "No matter how good our life was, something was always wrong. No matter what I felt, I wasn't able to be encouraging to him. I learned to keep a lid on my feelings, and after a while all I felt was numb. I felt guilty whenever I felt good because he didn't feel good. I quit listening to my feelings, and look at me now."

"What was your marriage like emotionally?"

"No matter what I felt, it was wrong. If I was happy, he couldn't understand why. And because nothing ever made him feel good, he never shared my happiness. If I was angry, he didn't think I had a right to feel angry. If I was discouraged, he thought I was being ridiculous. I came to see that nothing I felt would be right for him because he had convinced me that my emotions had no validity."

"I'm curious," I said. "Do you see any similarities between your husband's attitude and the attitudes of your family members when you were growing up?"

Sandy snickered.

"Are you kidding?" she said. "My mother is the ultimate crazy-maker. It's all about her. When she calls me she still dominates the conversation. I learned a long time ago that nothing I could do would make her happy and that she would never really care how I felt. She was great when it came to telling me how to feel and think about things, but she never asked for my opinion."

"What happened if you shared your feelings with her?"

"If I was upset, she'd tell me not to be upset. If I was happy, she would downplay whatever I was happy about."

"So first from your mother and then from your husband, you learned either not to listen to your feelings or to label them as good or bad."

Sandy clearly had a lot of unlearning to do.

Unlearning

We all have a lot of unlearning and relabeling to do. We have to give up unfair value judgments, the exclusion of God from our emotional lives, and arbitrary labels about our feelings. We must guard against the possibility of moralizing about our emotions—"I shouldn't be feeling this way"—which brings undue guilt and anxiety. Labeling feelings as right or wrong creates confusion, pulling us further away from our emotions and their decision-making possibilities. We need to open our minds to the possibility that our emotional life is actually a unique pathway to God.

Just as I learned to suppress anger and now must unlearn that, most of us have unlearning to do. Sandy had to unlearn the idea that her feelings don't matter. She had to be the first person to champion her emotions. She needed to accept that her feelings can help her make critical decisions. She is in the process of learning how to identify her feelings as well as name them.

Unlearning also helps us not to moralize our feelings. Consider Sandy's situation. She learned first from her mother and then from her husband that she was not to have any feelings. Thus, whenever she did have them, she felt guilty. Her emotions were, after all, apparently wrong. But she *did* experience those feelings, if only for a moment, and then became confused even more by them. They set off a chain reaction that led to a series of additional feelings that contributed to her confusion.

Therapists often say that a feeling denied is intensified. We cannot truly convince our core self that certain feelings are off-limits. We have them, and that's all there is to it. Try as we might to suppress certain emotions, we must acknowledge and own them before we can make much-needed changes.

Emotions Make Us Human

As Sandy suppressed her emotions, she became depressed. She lost parts of herself that made her a unique person. As she denied those unique qualities and emotions, she became discouraged and hopeless about finding the way out of her confusion. Her task in therapy included recovering her lost emotions.

Consider the power and helpfulness of recovering lost emotions. They empower us to do several critical things:

- become real and authentic people
- understand what is important to us and how to set boundaries with others
- become more intimate in our relationships because emotional vulnerability helps us to be intimate with others

- attend to what is happening now as we remember both positive and negative past experiences as part of the fabric of our lives
- add texture to our lives rather than oversimplifying things as right or wrong, good or bad
- develop a broader and richer vocabulary about our lives
- live mindfully, aware that all we have is this current moment
- enrich our worship, prayer, and contact with God

Carefully review this list. Would you really want to omit any of these aspects from your emotional life? You can see that each item is an integral aspect of our humanity. To deny even one is to deny part of who we are. No wonder some people live only from the neck up, without the emotional presence of their heart.

Our feelings are God-given, and this is a critical aspect of our humanity. Our emotions, perhaps more than anything else, make us who and what we are. Someone has said that we are not so much human beings trying to be spiritual as spiritual beings trying to be human.

All Emotion Is Useful

Every emotion can be useful, even if only to inform us that we need to attend to something or change our behavior. Emotions are also a wonderful starting place for contact with God. As we invite God into this most intimate part of our lives, we establish true contact with Him.

I shared in the opening chapter how my friend Craig overreacted to Jannine's recent trip to Wisconsin to see her brother. Her leaving awakened old feelings of sadness from his divorce. These were wounds he thought were completely healed, but obviously they needed more attention.

How was that sadness useful to Craig? How did those feelings allow him closer contact with God? As soon as he realized that he was still distressed and angry over being victimized in his marriage, he was able to honestly accept these feelings and attend to them. He took action to journal about them as well as seek short-term counseling to help him process these emotions. Attaching these feelings to their original and proper source helped him avoid attaching them inappropriately to Jannine.

Craig was tempted to label his sadness about his divorce as wrong. He had to reject assessments like these:

- You should be over your sadness. That happened six years ago.

- You can't be sad now. You're remarried. If Jannine finds out that you're still sad, she might think she can't make you happy.

- Something must be wrong with you to still feel such sadness.

- Feeling sad after all this time is a bad thing.

Can you hear how terribly unhelpful these thoughts are? Do you see how they create confusion by implying that he should be over certain feelings because of some arbitrary timeline? Such thinking would only serve to cause deeper problems for him.

In fact, those beliefs have already made matters worse for Craig. Regardless of what he tells himself, part of him believes he should be over his occasional sadness. He's suppressed his sorrow because he doesn't want to keep feeling sad. He wants to forget his old life and live fully in his new one. But life is not that simple.

No clear delineation line appears between his old life and his new one. His sadness helped him see that he still had some grief-related work to do.

When we reflexively label emotions as either good or bad, we surrender the possibility of properly attending to them and learning from them.

So let's say for now that feeling sad is all right. But what about feeling envious of others? That is an emotion I struggle with at times. Clearly, that feeling is wrong, right? Well, again, I prefer not to moralize too much about it. Rather, I try to learn what might be useful about that particular emotion, and I consider how to keep it from turning into an attitude of sinful covetousness.

So, what is useful about envy? Certainly envy leads quickly to sin, right? Well, not always. It can if we allow ourselves to wallow in the envy and to covet what others have. If we dwell on the blessings others enjoy, forgetting our own blessings, we can get into trouble. But the problem is with the decision we make, not the emotions we feel.

How has envy been a useful emotion for me? I have a bold and vivid imagination. Daydreaming about situations that I find appealing is not unusual for me. Here's an example.

As I write this chapter, we are in the midst of a dreary, cool winter. Some people don't mind the gray skies and damp weather, but I've grown to dislike them. Am I ungrateful for the Washington beauty? Not at all. I wouldn't live anywhere else. But when I hear of folks leaving our rainy winter for the sunny Southwest, I'm flat-out envious. When I hear their stories of eating outside on their decks in the balmy weather while I'm huddled indoors with the heater cranked full blast, I'm envious. They take evening walks while I dash through the drizzle from my car to my home under an umbrella, and I'm jealous.

But how is that emotion useful to me? It is useful because I realize that I have some decisions to make, and I want to make them honestly and with God's blessing. I want to listen to those feelings (which He gave me) without letting them rule me. My emotions tell me that I want to spend part of my vacation time in warmer climates. I need to leave the mood-dampening rain and get into the spirit-lifting sunshine. I don't think God minds at all that this is what

I want. This is a part of my nature, which I must attend to if I am to properly care for myself.

Having said this, we must make sure to assess all of our wants, desires, and emotions in the light of God's will for our lives as we understand it. We must be open to spiritual convictions that go against our simple desires. Then we can relax and consider our emotions on a particular matter—such as how to live with sunshine and rain.

I'm sure you can relate. Perhaps you'd rather not feel some emotions. You have probably labeled some feelings as wrong or bad, but they are neither. They can help you live the life God intended for you to live.

Hearing God

The Scriptures clearly state that God created us in His image. We are obviously not God, but we have many of His attributes, such as our mind, will, and emotions, and those provide us with the capacity for relationship with Him.

God speaks to us in our entirety, so if we deny our inner experience—our emotional life—we cut ourselves off from one method God uses to speak to us. This is like covering one ear when listening to our mate. We're not likely to get the full message.

Consider the fact that God speaks to us through our reading of the living Word, our time in prayer, our contact with other believers, our experiences, and our ongoing relationship with Him. This full relationship, enhanced by our emotional nature, helps us hear God. These are aspects of what the apostle John calls abiding in Jesus: "I am the vine; you are the branches. If a man remains in me and I in him, he will bear much fruit; apart from me you can do nothing" (John 15:5).

Ronald Dunn, in his book *Don't Just Stand There, Pray Something,* says, "Simply put, we are to be to Jesus what a branch is to the vine. As the branch abides in the vine, we are to abide in Jesus. Abide speaks of the union and communion between the vine and branches. To abide in Jesus is to live the life of a branch."[1]

Certainly, this kind of abiding suggests a sharing of our entire selves—our emotions, thoughts, and spiritual nature. *Abide* suggests a comprehensive relationship.

Just a few verses later, Jesus expands on this notion of abiding:

> Greater love has no one than this, that he lay down his life for his friends. You are my friends if you do what I command. I no longer call you servants, because a servant does not know his master's business. Instead, I have called you friends, for everything that I learned from my Father I have made known to you (John 15:13-15).

Jesus no longer considers us servants, but friends. This friendship certainly includes a mutual understanding of our inner selves, including our emotional lives.

Because Jesus is our friend, He surely wants to relate to us in our everyday experiences. Our lives are often filled with mundane struggles, not pious and holy experiences. Jesus wants to meet us where our lives intersect our experiences: in our emotions. Here, in the midst of our emotional experiences—the challenges with our boss, our anger with a neighbor, even a conflict with our mate—He is ready to help us. In the midst of our murky, confusing relationships, He is willing to provide counsel. We can count on Him to help us heal from emotional struggles, process our emotions, and move forward with life.

The Student Pastor

The issue of God caring about our everyday lives was evident when I talked to a young client recently concerning conflict with his girlfriend. Tim is a passionate man who is studying to be a pastor. He wants to honor God in everything he does and is determined to grow in his faith and in his fledgling love life. He struggles to understand what God is doing in this love relationship, so full of twists and turns that it makes his head spin. He wants to know if God is the author of the twists and turns or if He is simply there to abide with Tim on this bouncy road.

"How much of my restlessness is caused by God," Tim asked me, "and how much am I creating? It's driving me crazy."

Tim is straining to distinguish God's voice from his thoughts and the voice of his emotions.

"I go for a walk every day," Tim continued, "and every day I ask God what He wants me to do about my love life. If He wants me to stay with Jessica, why is it so difficult? Why are there so many challenges? I want to honor God in every part of my life, but my love life is so confusing."

"Let's talk about your concerns," I said.

"Maybe my relationship with Jessica isn't the issue. Maybe God is trying to get my attention. I want to know what He thinks about our relationship."

"I'm not sure what will happen with you and your girlfriend," I told him. "God wants you to abide with Him through the process, and He promises to give you wisdom. He just might give wisdom *through* your emotions."

"So does He want me to be with her or not?" he asked impatiently. "If I just had the answer to that question, everything else would be so easy."

"I don't know the answer," I said. "Sometimes we try too hard to manage the details. I think we should simply follow the prophet Micah, who said 'to act justly and to love mercy and to walk humbly with your God' (Micah 6:8). If you listen to your emotions and use the good reasoning God gave you, I'm sure you'll make wise decisions."

"I'm feeling very uncertain about this relationship. I don't know if that's coming from God or from me."

"I encourage you to listen to your uncertainty," I said. "As long as you're following Scripture, you're on pretty solid ground. As you listen to your emotions and prayerfully ask for wisdom, I believe you'll discover the best direction for your life."

We continued discussing the many worries he had about his girl-friend. He shared concerns about her not being of the same faith. He also told me that he believes she has problems managing her anger. He has come to realize that his uncertainty is a great barometer, indicating deeper problems in their relationship.

Tim is being obedient to God and trying to attend to his emotions. He's decided to move ahead slowly with his girlfriend and to talk with her about his concerns. He's also invited God into his emotional life and is much more peaceful about the decisions he is making.

Emotions That Clutter the Path

Not all emotions enhance our contact with God. Some clutter the path and actually keep us from making sound decisions. We sometimes allow ourselves to wallow in feelings and don't process them effectively. Volatile emotions can hinder us from hearing the voice of God.

Many biblical characters attended to their emotions and then made foolish choices. Consider King David and his infatuation with Bathsheba. He made one poor decision after another, leading to adultery and murder. Cain failed to manage his anger and murdered his brother. In a jealous rage, King Saul tried to kill David.

Bitterness often leads to problematic decisions. Consider what the apostle Paul says about this and other related emotions: "Get rid of all bitterness, rage and anger, brawling and slander, along with every form of malice. Be kind and compassionate to one another, forgiving each other, just as in Christ God forgave you" (Ephesians 4:31-32). Bitterness settles into our hearts and affects the way we view others, God, and even ourselves. It creates a toxic spirit that hinders our relationship with God.

Maintaining an attitude of bitterness is no easy thing. Like resent-ment, which we will explore at length in another chapter, bitterness requires that we dwell on some real or imaginary injustice. To maintain resentment and bitterness, we must restrict our vision and narrow our thoughts, seeing ourselves as victims and others as villains. We nurse a grudge and make decisions that we suppose will help us get even. These emotions and behaviors separate us from God.

The apostle Paul saw people living in conflict with one another. He watched as backbiting, bitterness, and anger took their toll on relationships. That is why he challenged everyone to "speak to one another with psalms, hymns and spiritual songs...Submit to one another out of reverence for Christ" (Ephesians 5:19,21). He knew that keeping channels clear with others would also keep the pathway open to God.

The Usefulness of Bitterness

Who of us hasn't felt bitterness toward someone? Most of us can quickly think of someone we've resented. We may have nurtured that resentment until it became full-blown hostility.

We all slip easily into bitterness, so we need to explore ways to use this challenging emotion to create positive experiences. We can partner with God to use bitterness so we come out in a healthier place. But to do that, we need to keep several things in mind.

Bitterness is like a spiked fever, pointing to a serious problem. A fever gets our attention. We think of little else when we are in that kind of misery. The same is true of bitterness. This feeling stems from the lack of forgiveness in our hearts and consumes us until we can think of little else. Hurt and sadness are normal, but choosing to let rage germinate within us is sinful and leads to debilitating bitterness. With a minimum of reflection, we can usually discover the source of our problem. If we take responsibility for those feelings and don't blame others for our misery, we can often determine how to change our attitude or address unresolved issues we have with others and experience deep healing.

Search deep to discover the real source of your pain. Rather than running away from your anguish by launching into a tirade against that person who betrayed you or that loved one who neglected you, look inside for that hurt little girl or boy needing love. Ask the Lord to come alongside that wounded little child and love him or her unconditionally.

Feeling hurt by injustice is natural. However, while hurt and anger can be healthy emotions, bitterness is typically not productive. Explore whether other emotions, such as hurt and anger, are hidden beneath the bitterness. Take an emotional inventory to see what other emotions may be lying below the surface. Attend to them and explore healthier decisions.

Be ready to find echoes of the current issue earlier in your life. Expect to discover similar problems that you haven't dealt with effectively. Prepare to unearth wounds that haven't healed and that need tender loving from God and from yourself. Ask Him to elucidate those areas of your life where you are hanging on to old wounds.

Bitterness is a profound opportunity for healing. You can make a decision, based on this emotion, to invite God into your heart to change not only your feelings but also the thoughts that lead up to these destructive emotions.

Weighing Our Emotions

Emotions can overwhelm us. They can sneak up on us and create moods. Who of us hasn't been overcome by a disposition but not known how it originated? Such can be the wily ways of our emotions. Because of this, our feelings should never be our only guide as we determine a course of action. As I've said, emotions are useful in decision making, but we should not rely solely on them. Wise people temper their feelings with sound decision making.

The Scriptures warn us not to be deceived. "There is a way that seems right to a man, but in the end it leads to death" (Proverbs 16:25). "All of a man's ways seem right to him, but the Lord weighs the heart" (Proverbs 21:2).

Understanding our emotions and working to keep them in balance are critical. Hurt run amok turns into bitterness. We must manage our emotions just as we manage our thought life. "We demolish arguments and every pretension that sets itself up against the knowledge of God, and we take captive every thought to make it obedient to Christ" (2 Corinthians 10:5).

Our emotions are inextricably linked to our thoughts—our thinking gives way to our emotions—so we need to practice keeping our thought life balanced. As the apostle Paul said, we can be transformed by the renewing of our minds (Romans 12:2).

We are mind-body-spirit beings, and each part affects the others. Just as a weary body can lead to depression, rampant emotions can damage the body, and spiritual malaise can affect both the mind and body. The challenge is to keep each part of our nature in balance.

Inviting God into Our Emotions

Certainly, we want to make good decisions about our emotions. To allow hurt to lead to resentment and then to bitterness is to let emotions run out of control. We know that Jesus was angry, and yet He didn't sin. We want to follow His example.

Emotions, calm or stormy, provide powerful opportunities to invite God into the everyday issues of our lives. As we name and embrace our feelings and refuse to label them as good or bad, we accept our frail humanity and allow God to work powerfully in our lives.

Brennan Manning, in his wonderful book *The Ragamuffin Gospel,* speaks plainly about the joys and challenges of living the Christian life. He is no sanctimonious preacher but rather a fallen straggler in need of God's grace. He comforts us in our emotionally volatile lives:

> To those of us in flight, who are afraid to turn around lest we run into ourselves, Jesus says, "You have a home...I am your home...you will find it to be the intimate place where I have found my home...it is right where you are...in your innermost being...in your heart."[2]

The issue is not whether our emotions are godly, but rather

whether we are willing to invite God into all our thoughts and emotions on a daily basis. He, through the work of the indwelling Holy Spirit, suffers as we suffer and experiences our emotions along with us. If we invite Him into our everyday experiences, we will, more often than not, make healthy decisions. If we allow Christ to be at home in our hearts, we will live with His abiding grace, and that will change us for the better. Our emotions provide myriad opportunities to partner with God as He transforms us.

Join me as we now look at the power of denial to stop us from fully utilizing emotional decision making.

4

Denial Is Not a River in Egypt

If ignorance is bliss, you must be ecstatic.

UNKNOWN

I recently read about a young woman who had an abnormal mammogram. After taking a thorough history and performing a battery of tests, her physician determined that she was suffering from late-stage breast cancer and that she had some idea of her condition. The malignant tumor had metastasized to other organs, and her condition was so poor that she died a short time after her initial visit to the doctor.

Stories like this leave doctors shaking their heads in disbelief. What is going on in patients' minds when they allow a condition to worsen instead of getting treatment?

But scenes like this happen every day. Doctors commonly see situations in which patients delay reporting physical problems. Many people refuse to take care of themselves and then deny the severity of their condition, even in light of compelling evidence to the contrary.

The woman had to be experiencing significant discomfort, which she apparently did her best to deny. She must have hidden her discomfort from her immediate family and close friends. She had to have been very creative in rationalizing her denial. But it led to her premature death. This woman ignored information that might have led to her recovery.

Impossible, you say? No. Unusual? Definitely not. Denial is powerful in the physical realm and in the spiritual and emotional domains as well. Denial can protect us, but it also has the power to kill us—literally.

On a regular basis, I see advanced stages of emotional issues that people could have avoided if they had simply listened to their feelings and acknowledged them. Like physical symptoms, emotions—which are a pathway to God and to our innermost being—require our attention. As we've discovered, emotions are essential to understanding what is important to us. They warn us, inform us, and make us human. We deny our emotions at our own physical, emotional, and spiritual peril.

Inside Denial

I didn't know the woman who delayed reporting her symptoms and subsequently died, and I have little idea as to her thinking prior to her premature death. I can, however, imagine what might have been going through her mind. Walk into this imaginary world with me, where I allow an imaginary doctor to interview her. As you listen to this interview, consider that her distorted thinking may be similar to our own.

> Doctor: "Why did you wait so long before coming to see me?"
> Woman: "I hoped the pain would go away. I didn't want to make something out of nothing."
> Doctor: "But your family history shows a high incidence of breast cancer. Didn't that alert you to the possibility that it might be something more serious?"
> Woman: "Well, yes and no. I hoped that it wasn't bad news. I didn't want to face the possibility that the same disease that took my mother's life might take mine."
> Doctor: "You didn't want to face the challenges of cancer?"
> Woman: "Exactly. I thought about what it would be like a

few times, but then I blocked it out of my mind. That made me feel much better. It's pretty simple, really."

Doctor: "But what about your symptoms? What about the lump on your breast? What about the pain in your chest?"

Woman: "Yes, they were there. But I was able to distract myself from those problems. I'm an active person, and I told myself I should ignore the symptoms and get on with my life."

Doctor: "Even though the disease was killing you?"

Woman: "I didn't tell myself the disease was killing me. In fact, I told myself I was fine, and that all of this would pass."

I can easily imagine how the woman might answer because I am very familiar with denial. In fact, we're all acquainted with denial; it's a universal phenomenon. All of us, to some extent, block out deadly symptoms, avoid healing thoughts and beliefs, and ignore the truth. We block out emotions even though they clearly point to danger.

Before being too critical of this woman and the convoluted thinking that led to her inaction and early death, we should admit that her inaction is similar to our inaction, her avoidance is similar to our avoidance, and her death is similar to the small deaths we experience every day because we refuse to listen to our heart, soul, mind, and emotions.

This is the power of denial. It is a profound force, capable of wreaking destruction. It can protect us, but it is so potent that until we acknowledge that we each have the ability to deny, we cannot change the course of our lives for the better. If we are going to embrace the power of emotional decision making, we must confront the power of denial.

Defining Denial

We all use denial, and sometimes that's a good thing. We could never face all that comes our way in one fell swoop. For that reason, we utilize denial to help us cope with things that feel overwhelming.

Think of denial as rose-colored glasses we use to see things a certain way. John Bradshaw, in his book *Healing the Shame That Binds You*, describes denial this way: "Perhaps the most elementary ego defense is denial. In the face of a threat, people deny what is going on, or they deny the hurt of what is going on, or the impact on their lives of what is going on."[1]

Denial protects us from things we feel we cannot cope with. This may save us from immediate anxiety or pain, but denial requires a substantial investment of energy. Because of this, we use other defenses to keep these unacceptable feelings away. Let's consider some situations we commonly deny:

- *Death.* Upon hearing news of a friend's or family member's death, we may deny the news and insist there must be some mistake. The more important the relationship, the greater the dependency on the lost person, and the greater the likelihood for denial.

- *Severe sickness.* Many people, upon hearing of their grave or terminal illness, deny its presence. The news is too much to incorporate, so they opt for temporary or even permanent denial.

- *Rejection.* No one wants to feel unloved or unwanted. We often deny our personal responsibility in situations where we are rejected. We commonly attack the rejecter rather than honestly face the circumstances that led to the broken relationship.

- *Relationship difficulties.* Just as with physical maladies, many people want to deny relationship sickness. Couples often wait until their relationship is in dire straits before they seek counseling. Many choose to put their heads in the sand, hoping the problems will magically resolve themselves.

These are just a few of the many problems that prompt an emotional response of denial. Any situation that overwhelms our ability to effectively respond may lead to this condition. Let's now look at how denial impacted the emotional decision making of one couple in distress.

Denial and Decisions

I'm currently working with a couple who appear to be caught in the labyrinth of denial. Cynthia and Curt have been married for ten years and came to see me in an effort to save their marriage. I was excited to begin working with this vibrant couple with two young children.

Cynthia is a spritely woman with a quick sense of humor. She offers biblical aphorisms and shares her strong desire for a godly marriage. Curt is more laid-back and is not as excited about the counseling process. Yet when I asked about his motivation, he shared a sincere desire to solve their problems.

My first clue that things were not exactly as they seemed came when Curt and Cynthia told me that they had been having problems for years but that they had never sought counseling from a professional or even advice from friends.

"We've been having problems from the start of our marriage," Cynthia said. "We nitpick with each other and then wonder why we don't feel close to each other. But I just figured that things would get better."

"You never thought about getting help?" I asked.

"Well, not seriously," she said. "We're both busy with our jobs, and the girls take up a lot of our time. I've told myself not to be jealous, but every once in a while I can't help it."

"Jealous?" I asked.

"Yeah," she said, eyeing Curt. "I don't know if he's completely committed to me or if he checks out other women when I'm not around."

"How about you, Curt?" I asked. "Did you ever think about getting help?"

"I'm not really into counseling, and I'm not sure the problem is as big as she thinks. I've never heard that counseling helped anybody. Besides, things between us aren't that bad."

I watched as Cynthia raised her eyebrows and shrugged.

"Aren't things pretty bad right now?" I asked.

"They're about the same as they've always been," Cynthia shrugged. "Except I caught Curt flirting with another woman at work, and I'm not sure he hasn't been cheating on me for some time."

"Not true," Curt said sharply. "That's just not true. I haven't done anything that I haven't been doing for ten years. I'm a bit of a flirt, but that's all there is to it."

As the session progressed, the seriousness of their problems became increasingly clear. Yet they remained somewhat detached. I was watching a couple die emotionally and spiritually, yet they were seemingly unaware of the extreme danger they were in.

How could Curt and Cynthia ignore the emotional and relational disease in their marriage? Why does a catastrophe have to happen before people become aware?

Denial.

If emotional awareness heals and helps us make healthy and effective decisions, denial blocks those positive processes. If tuning in to our emotions, learning to embrace and name them, heals as God speaks to us, denial silences those powerful messages.

Temptation and Denial

With so much to lose, you'd think we'd all be fighting to embrace the truth in our lives. We can't make illness go away by closing our eyes, nor can we make marital distress vanish by wishing it away. However, we face a huge temptation to slip into denial because of its many apparent benefits.

First, by denying what's happening, we can deny the impact of that event on our lives. The woman with cancer was able, for a time, to deny that the illness had permeated her body. She lived as if she were in good health, pretending that if she didn't acknowledge her illness, she wouldn't have to acknowledge the impact of the illness on her life. Curt and Cynthia lived as if their relationship were in good health, all the while sensing that perhaps this was not true.

Second, pretending that the problem doesn't exist is a way to manage our fears. When fear begins to overwhelm us, we may use denial to cope. When we feel particularly vulnerable, we use denial to push unwanted emotions away—at least temporarily. This allows us to breathe a sigh of relief as if the problem were solved.

Third, denying a problem allows us to maintain the illusion of invincibility. Who wants to believe that harm might befall them? Who wouldn't rather pretend they will live forever? Denial allows us to live in this fantasy world.

Fourth, denying a problem allows us to escape personal responsibility for our lives. When I convince myself that I am overwhelmed by life's circumstances, denial allows me to live as if I can't do anything about them. It also allows me to believe that I haven't caused this predicament. Denial gives me permission to live passively. I am protected in this fairy-tale world and excused from making difficult decisions, facing painful and challenging feelings, or taking responsibility for my life.

The Benefits of Short-Term Denial

Long-term denial is debilitating, but short-term denial can be helpful.

First, short-term denial gives us time to marshal resources to cope with a traumatic event. Sometimes all we need is a little time to sit back and reflect on the situation before making decisions. A little time gives us the opportunity to sort through myriad feelings, letting the reality of a situation slowly settle in.

Second, short-term denial allows us time to face our fears and other unpleasant emotions. If we've been accustomed to keeping our emotions in check, a little time allows us to consider our feelings and make decisions about them. Simply spending some time with our feelings is often all that we need to soothe them.

Third, short-term denial allows us time to accept the reality of the situation. If something is too big to swallow in one bite, we might be able to digest it bit by bit. Slowly, we are able to accept that something big has happened to us. We are able to sit with the immensity of the problem and then prepare to make adjustments.

Fourth, short-term denial gives us time to restructure our lives to accommodate this new information. If there is a major death in our family, we need time to reflect on life without our loved one. If a major illness has struck us or someone we love, we need time to consider what life will be like with this change of health. Regardless of the type of loss, we need to reflect and accommodate it into our lives. Time is necessary if we are to determine how this problem will affect us so we can make the required adjustments.

Denial Can Weaken Us

Rather than making us stronger and more resilient, long-term denial ultimately weakens us. Seeing our problems as too big to manage makes them seem more overwhelming than they really are. Rather than facing our troubles and becoming more effective at dealing with them, denial says, in effect, "These problems are too much for me. I'm too weak to face them. I'll put my head in the sand and pretend they don't exist." We usually need to be more realistic about the size of our problems and our ability to handle them.

My wife is deathly afraid of mice. Not just mice scampering beneath our house or in the rafters, but even dead mice caught in one of my traps. Even though she knows the dead mouse cannot harm her, she feels as if it might magically jump out of the trap and attack her.

Subsequently, I'm always on a mouse hunt, always clearing the way for her to go into our basement unscathed. This is a silly example, but you may be able to relate. Her fears are unreasonable, but because of her denial that the mouse can't hurt her, she shrinks from her otherwise normal activities.

In many cases, we deny our ability to face a fantasized adversary and allow our fears to grow. While we are in the midst of denial, our problems worsen. We cannot wink and expect our problems to simply maintain the status quo. Even though we feel inadequate to deal effectively with them, denial won't make our troubles vanish. If anything, they grow, so the denial we use to keep our problems at bay actually makes them larger.

The stronger and larger our problems become, the more inadequate we feel to face them. But stalling, avoiding, and shifting our focus are not useful strategies. The problems will still be there when the denial fades.

We may also get in the habit of using magical thinking. If we deny our emotions in one part of life, chances are that we'll be tempted to deny them in other areas as well. Delusional thinking or denial often leads to interpersonal problems. Some people are willing to face their troubles and underlying emotions, but others seem unwilling or unable to do so. This difference can lead to conflict. Denial of reality is irrational and childlike, so we can expect people in denial to experience conflict with those who are able to face reality.

When we habitually use denial, we fail to practice emotional decision making. Our emotional decision-making muscles atrophy, and we become less effective decision makers. The opposite is also true. When we practice tuning into our emotions and making effective emotional choices, our decision-making muscles grow strong.

Facing the Truth

Denial makes us weak, but facing our emotions and our problems makes us strong. As James, the half-brother of Jesus, said, "Consider it pure joy, my brothers, whenever you face trials of many kinds, because you know that the testing of your faith develops perseverance.

Perseverance must finish its work so that you may be mature and complete, not lacking anything" (James 1:2-4).

These truths shouldn't surprise us, but they are often much easier said than done. Scott Peck, author of the renowned book *The Road Less Traveled,* has much to say about the importance of telling ourselves and others the truth.

> Dealing with the pain of problem-solving, which must continually be employed if our lives are to be healthy and our spirits are to grow, is dedication to the truth...The more clearly we see the reality of the world, the better equipped we are to deal with the world. The less clearly we see the reality of the world—the more our minds are befuddled by falsehood, misperceptions and illusions—the less able we will be to determine correct courses of action and make wise decisions.[2]

The most obvious course of action is to face reality. It is a way to tackle the thorniest problems, to accept the most uncomfortable feelings, and to join forces with others who are also willing to face the truth.

But this isn't the path most people take. When we face new information that is unpleasant and threatening, all but the strongest of us find ways to discount it. When we experience feelings we haven't felt in ages, all but the most courageous find ways to suppress them, discount them, project them, or ingeniously avoid them. Facing the truth is not nearly as easy as some people make it sound.

Peck states that dedication to the truth includes stringent self-examination. Dedication to the truth requires a willingness to be personally challenged. The only way to be certain that our map of reality is accurate, he says, is to expose it to criticism and challenge.

So we should share not only our intellectual view of the world but also our emotional one. The most honest conversation is not only heady with perceptions but also emotional, involving our gut-level reactions to the world. When we share how situations truly affect us on an emotional level, we become vulnerable, sharing our most intimate self.

Julia Cameron, author of the book *The Artist's Way,* believes that breaking down denial is necessary for recovering a sense of integrity. She asserts that we have "official" feelings, those we share with the public, and "real" feelings, which we often keep secret. "At the root of a successful creative recovery is the commitment to puncture our denial, to stop saying, 'It's okay' when in fact it's something else."[3] Cameron suggests that finding our personal truths requires considerable self-examination. She recommends journaling every day in order to discover our truest self.

> Over any considerable period of time, the morning pages [journaling] perform spiritual chiropractic. They realign our values. If we are to the left or the right of our personal truth, the pages will point out the need for a course adjustment. We will become aware of our drift and correct it—if only to hush the pages up. "To thine own self be true," the pages say, while busily pointing the self out.[4]

Following Cameron's advice, I began journaling many years ago. Journaling has been a powerful tool in breaking through my denial and facing painful truths. Through journaling, I've come to realize that I, like others, am invariably in the process of giving birth to new feelings of excitement and joy while grieving things that are dying. Solomon noted the same thing when he said, "To everything there is a season" (Ecclesiastes 3:1 NKJV).

Without journaling, I could easily remain in denial about these subtle changes. By reading Scripture, praying, and journaling, I've made many discoveries: my calling to a life as a writer, my love for my home and life on Puget Sound, my appreciation for my wife and her emerging gifts, my feelings of loss because my sons no longer live nearby, my adjustments with my counseling practice, my desire to be settled into our new church, and my feelings of confusion about where God is leading me in this area of my life.

I have powerful feelings associated with each of these situations. When I neglect journaling and reflection, I slip into denial about the impact each has on my life. They become undercurrents, impacting me in ways I am not fully aware of. However, when I acknowledge these forces, allowing the feelings to wash over me, I can embrace the feelings and engage in what I've been describing as emotional decision making.

As I mentioned, one of my greatest concerns is that my two grown sons live in New York. Most of the time, I am content, knowing that they are doing well in their medical schooling and are fine Christian men. I lull myself into thinking that I am okay with this. But if I am honest with myself, that is not the case.

Still, when when I am honest with myself, I know I can share things on the phone more frequently. I can tell them about the latest coffee shop I discovered in Seattle and ask about their latest outings. I can ask about the seasons of their lives in New York.

Listening carefully to my emotions helps me. Conversely, denial hurts me. Facing reality helps me make choices that fit closely with my personal values. Denying what is critically important in my life causes me to lose touch with myself, and I feel distant, detached, and discouraged. That's not the way I want to live.

More About Honesty

Sometimes being honest with ourselves seems trivial. This is the feeling I get when I read the memoirs of Anne Lamott or Nora Ephron.

Nora Ephron's recent title *I Feel Bad About My Neck* might at first seem ridiculous. But she is candid and forthright about something very important to her. How often do you hear someone tell the truth about how they feel about a part of their anatomy? Here's how she opens the book:

> I feel bad about my neck. Truly I do. If you saw my
> neck, you might feel bad about it too, but you'd probably

be too polite to let on. If I said something on the subject— something like "I absolutely cannot stand my neck"—you'd undoubtedly respond by saying something nice, like "I don't know what you're talking about." You'd be lying, of course, but I forgive you.[5]

Notice that Ephron introduces a topic no one ever talks about— their sagging neck—but which many think about, and she announces her feelings to hundreds of thousands of readers. And we're interested! She has the courage to talk about something so mundane yet so powerfully real to her.

Ephron continues her honest approach as she describes how she hates her purse, her hair, her landlord, and many other aspects of her life. She isn't depressed or depressing—just honest. And we can relate, which is the real point of the book. I find myself attracted more and more to authors and people who are willing to be honest, to step out of their nice, sanitized Christian roles and be real. That's the kind of person I am striving to be.

Being honest about our feelings is no less arduous than being honest about our lives. Robert Pasick, in his book *Awakening from the Deep Sleep*, talks about the importance of becoming honest with our feelings. This, he asserts, is the opposite of denial. It is discovering the truth about what is really taking place emotionally. Though written primarily for men, his book contains wisdom that is applicable for all.

> We have been raised to distrust our feelings. At an early age we were taught that to show emotional vulnerability was a sign of weakness…We rarely trust the emotional cues available to us. Instead we follow the blueprint that society provides to determine what we need and want—a good job, possessions, prestige, and power, all earned through hard work and preferably without complaints.[6]

Pasick illustrates the many ways we live dishonestly—in denial of our true feelings. He says we have become adept at hiding our true emotions. We talk about feeling good or bad, but rarely are we able to distinguish our exact feelings. He says that to perfect the denial of our feelings, we learn to attack others, shift blame, subvert our emotions, and even manipulate our facial muscles. We don't want to let on that we have feelings.

Living dishonestly creates serious consequences. We learn to distrust our inner experiences, and we don't learn to name and embrace our emotions. We live in a constant state of confusion about what we're actually feeling. Most importantly, we never learn the language for expressing feelings. In short, we live in denial.

This denial doesn't just affect *us,* of course. As a consequence of trying to manipulate my own feelings, I become less sensitive to the feelings of others. If I fail to attend to my feelings and inner experience, I won't be the best attendant to the feelings and needs of those around me. If I fail to make room for my own world of emotions, I won't be likely to create a safe place for the feelings and needs of my family and friends. The ripple effect of denial extends a long way.

Stages of Denial

Emerging from a state of denial isn't easy. Much has been written about the stages of grief since Elizabeth Kubler-Ross wrote her now-famous book *On Death and Dying.* She described five stages of grief: denial, anger, bargaining, depression, and finally acceptance.

Kubler-Ross stressed that we don't move through these stages in an orderly fashion. Rather, we shift back and forth between the stages many times. People commonly move out of denial and into anger, for example, and then back into denial for a time. They also commonly reach some level of acceptance, only to feel it slip out from under them as they feel intense anger again.

Talk to anyone about a significant loss in his life, and he'll tell you he felt sure he was over it when, perhaps quite suddenly, he was struck with grief again. These "sneaker waves" can make one feel as if the loss is as fresh today as it was months or years ago.

As we saw in the first chapter, my friend Craig certainly found this to be true regarding his divorce. Just when he thought he was completely finished grieving that loss, a sneaker wave knocked his legs out from under him. An old song, a favorite movie, or a special restaurant takes him back to the divorce and the problems that led up to it. But he practices what I've been preaching—being with his feelings. He lets them percolate to the surface, and soon they dissipate.

Coming out of denial is much the same. Many of us are reluctant to feel the immensity of a loss, to feel all the feelings associated with some challenging event in our lives. However, you can't heal what you can't feel. The only way out of something is to go through it, attending to each stage of grief and loss. Those feelings apply to small losses as much as they do to larger ones. A loss is a loss. Feeling whatever you feel is what is important, and it's the surest way through a difficult situation and an effective pathway to making healthy decisions.

Jesus and the Truth

The only perfect truth teller is Jesus. The rest of us straddle the fence between acceptance and denial, mincing words and telling little white lies. We live in fantasy one day and reality the next. Although most of us, thankfully, are never completely lost in a fantasy world, we often have more than a little rose-colored tint to our worldview.

Jesus is the exception. He tells it the way it is. Always motivated by love, He tells us the truth by which we can map out our world. This truth can lead us out of self-deception and denial and into the freedom that comes with knowing the truth. "The truth shall set you free," He said (John 8:32).

Facing His imminent death, Jesus spent His final hours with His disciples. When He might have hidden away, physically or emotionally, when He could have immersed Himself in denial, He faced the ultimate, horrific truth. Mark describes the scene in his Gospel:

> They went to a place called Gethsemane, and Jesus said to his disciples, "Sit here while I pray." He took Peter, James and John along with him, and he began to be deeply distressed and troubled. "My soul is overwhelmed with sorrow to the point of death," he said to them. "Stay here and keep watch."
>
> Going a little farther, he fell to the ground and prayed that if possible the hour might pass from him. "Abba, Father," he said, "everything is possible for you. Take this cup from me. Yet not what I will, but what you will." Then he returned to his disciples and found them sleeping (Mark 14:32-36).

The passage is rich with suspense and emotion. Jesus wanted and needed His friends to support Him in the midst of His agony. He didn't try to hide His pain and anguish. He pleaded with the Father, asking if He needed to proceed with the plan that would lead to His death. The Scripture says He was overwhelmed with emotion, and He shared His struggle with His disciples and His heavenly Father. Philip Yancey makes this comment in his book *The Jesus I Never Knew:*

> By instinct, we humans want someone by our side in the hospital the night before surgery, in the nursing home as death looms near, in any great moment of crisis. We need the reassuring touch of human presence—solitary confinement is the worst punishment our species has devised. I detect in the Gospel's account of Gethsemane a profound depth of loneliness that Jesus had never before encountered.[7]

This is a revealing picture of the humanity of Jesus and encourages us to share our struggles with Him. The story emboldens us to feel all of our emotions honestly. None will surprise or frighten Him.

The story also entices us to come out of denial about our feelings and to face them honestly. Only by facing our emotions honestly and inviting God into them can we make the wisest decisions.

5

The Gifts of Irritability and Frustration

What annoyances are more painful
than those of which we cannot complain?

Marquis de Custine

After a long day at the office, I decided to stop by the grocery store for a few dinner ingredients. I encountered a lot of harried, unfriendly shoppers who cut in front of me, wheeling carts around like Indianapolis 500 drivers, each intent on getting his or her shopping done with little regard for anyone else's feelings.

Bumper-to-bumper rush-hour traffic only added to my aggravation as I crawled home. Road rage, or at least road tension, was definitely in the air.

By the time I walked in the door, I was down. The shoppers bugged me, the drivers bugged me, and my wife bugged me—and she hadn't even done anything wrong!

Christie greeted me pleasantly and then continued with her schoolwork. Later, when she attempted to chat with me, everything she said seemed to catch an edge in my soul and rub me raw. I did my best not to growl at her, knowing that she wasn't out of sorts. I was.

She didn't take long to figure out I was irritable. I don't hide those things well. Setting aside her work, she walked over to me and reached out for my hand.

"What's the matter, David? Bad day at the office?"

"Not really," I groused. "Just a bunch of little things setting me off."

"What can I do to help?"

I started to calm down. Christie's gentleness was like a warm, soothing shower after a long, cold run.

"Maybe I just need to sit and relax with you for a few minutes."

"You've got it," she said. I spent the next 20 minutes sharing my frustrations. I talked about the challenges in my counseling practice, particularly the adolescent I had to hospitalize because of his suicidal feelings. I shared the anger and inadequacy I felt at a deposition where I was challenged by the defense attorney in a child custody case. Finally, I talked about the insensitivities of some of the shoppers and drivers on the way home.

"Are you sure you want to keep handling child custody cases?" she asked. "The attorneys are pretty rough on you."

"I seem more upset afterward?"

"You seem angrier and more irritable than usual," she said. "It might be something to think about."

"They're very challenging, and I always get grilled when doing those cases. The courtroom is not an easy place to be," I said, aware that I was growing tighter as I talked about it.

"You don't seem to enjoy that kind of work anymore."

"I think you're right," I conceded. "I haven't really taken the time to consider whether that's how I want to be spending my professional time."

"Nothing is worth it if it makes you angry and frustrated, David. This is something you can change, and I suggest you take another look at the whole thing."

Nothing like a new perspective. My frustration and irritability were teaching me something very positive.

Attention and Safe Places

Christie provided a powerful antidote to my frayed nerves—the gift of her attention. She noticed my irritability and responded with concern. She could have become defensive or angry. Instead, she chose to offer me a safe place where I could discuss what was bothering me. She saw my tense emotions as symptoms of deeper issues and responded with tender care. Christie provided the gift of hospitality for my tensions, and I immediately felt better.

Christie offered something I probably wouldn't have given myself. What would I have done had she not been home? I might have journaled, which would have given me a hospitable place for my frayed emotions. Journaling would have given me an opportunity to distance myself from my troubling experiences. More likely, however, I would have ignored my feelings and simply gone through the motions that evening, allowing tension to smolder within and to erupt some time later.

The gift of providing attention, hospitality, and a safe haven for our emotions is powerful. Sometimes we don't need answers; we only need someone who is willing to listen while we vent. We need to complain about the pushy shoppers, the screaming babies, and the rush of testy people. We need to vent our frustration about the drivers who dart in and out of lanes as if they are in a race to the finish line.

Susan Ariel Rainbow Kennedy, known by her acronym, SARK, and author of *The Bodacious Book of Succulence,* is an ambassador for pampering the Self. She believes we all rush madly about in this world, gathering stress along the way, and forget to practice simple ways to drain off that tension. Her unabashed, self-indulgent message is incredibly simple and profound: Take care of your Self because no one else will do it the way you can and must. Take frequent naps, find the work you love, seek and give love generously. The first and most powerful way to accomplish this is to attend to your Self.

Irritability and frustration are most often emotions that simply say, "My battery is low and needs recharging. Give me a little TLC, and I can conquer the world again. Give me a nap and then a bowl of split pea soup, and I'm good for another round."

Soulful Listening

Christie provided attention, hospitality, and a safe place to emote. By the time she'd finished giving me a neck rub, I was good for another run at the world. More than anything else, I appreciated the fact that she took the time to really listen to what was bothering me.

Listening is one of the highest forms of love. It requires a safe environment conducive to communication. If I am to share my emotions with you, I must know that you won't judge my feelings, try to rescue me, or attempt to diminish my problems.

Christie did more than simply allow me to vent. She saw beneath my angry facade and noted something critically important—that I have been irritable after court many times. She sensed that I increasingly seem to dread the bickering and aggressiveness of the courtroom. She listened as I explained that I felt inadequate after being ripped by the defense attorney and as I wondered aloud whether the pay was worth the beating.

Notice that Christie didn't tell me what to do. She didn't tell me to stop doing this kind of work because she knows that I enjoy matching wits with defense attorneys. She didn't scold me. She simply provided an observation.

Christie looked beneath the surface of my irritability. She could see that it was like a fever, indicating something was amiss. She encouraged me to attend to my own discomfort and to consider using my bad temper to make healthy decisions for myself in the future.

In her fascinating book *Spiritual Housecleaning,* Kathryn Robyn says we need to construct a literal environment, a safe place where we can effectively attend to our feelings. She writes about creating a sacred space so these feelings can safely emerge. Just as we dust the corners of our homes, we must find ways to fashion an environment where we can dust the corners of our souls. When we create that kind of space, we are able to take inventory of the stresses and strains that impact our lives.

Robyn encourages us to clean house, literally and then figuratively. In a clean environment where we can spill our guts, we can learn a lot about what's bugging us. Robyn advises us to use the three Rs—which are closely related to emotional decision making:

- *Record* what you feel,
- *report* what you learn, and
- *respond* to your needs as they arise.

> Remember you are creating more *living* room for you and your soul. You may be reacquainting yourself with parts of yourself that have been forgotten or lost in the bustle of living. Now you are making room for those parts of yourself again, if only to dust them off and see if they are still you.[1]

I concur heartily. I clearly see how high-stress shopping, driving, working, and living clutter my life and create a breeding ground for irritability. When will I consider how the hostile courtroom is impacting me or ponder how the suicidal adolescent affects me? Where and when will I talk about how I feel knowing this young boy may one day succeed in killing himself? The answer lies in both my aggravation and a considerate wife who offers me a safe and sacred space to breathe, to be, and to become someone more than I am today.

The Hidden Voices of Irritability

Technically, irritability is not a feeling but an excessive response to an otherwise harmless, nonreactive situation. In other words, it is a signal that more is brewing beneath the surface. Or, as in my case, it may indicate a layering of frustrations. Many different sources can aggravate such a response, including medical conditions, lack of sleep, tiredness, poor nutrition, and of course, stress. Irritability usually occurs when frustrations mount or other feelings go unexpressed.

Irritability is an emotional response to feeling frustrated again and again. Irritability is always more than just irritability. It is a warning, an alarm demanding action. We inevitably harm ourselves when we attempt to suppress it. When we silence these symptoms of inner pain, we temporarily deny them, only to have them erupt again later, perhaps uncontrollably.

Irritability has many hidden and useful voices. Listen to all the possible voices percolating just beneath the surface on that evening with Christie.

- *You're saddened by the hospitalization of the youth and frightened by the destructive choices he may make in the future.*

- *You're frustrated with the attorney for ridiculing your testimony and your professional opinion.*

- *You're feeling anxious and rushed by the busy, insensitive people around you.*

- *You're upset for pushing yourself so hard. You need to slow down, relax, take a hot bath, and unwind.*

- *You need to be gently nurtured by your wife. You need to ask her for exactly what you need.*

Thankfully, I listened to these voices and took my own counsel. I recorded what I felt, reported what I learned, and responded with appropriate action. I took a wonderfully healing step that evening by asking Christie to talk with me, though I have more work to do. I still have some difficult decisions to make based on my recurring emotions, such as whether or not to continue doing court work, as well as finding ways to find and maintain the support I need if I am to handle the difficult aspects of being a psychologist.

My frustrations are very useful to me if I listen to them. I'm learning the importance of sharing with Christie my concerns about some of my clients and about the kinds of referrals I accept. My emotions are great resources for assisting me in making healthy decisions.

The Irritable Man

Kevin came to me as the result of a referral from his pastor. Kevin's wife had asked him to leave their home several months earlier because of his petulance and impatience.

Kevin sat in my waiting room with his chin resting on his hand, sullen and unapproachable. When I greeted him, Kevin offered a weak handshake and walked stiffly to my office. He was a large man, 53 years old, wearing denim jeans, a long-sleeve work shirt, and work boots.

After introducing myself, I asked Kevin to tell me why his pastor had sent him to see me.

"Seems my problems are big enough for my wife to kick me out," he offered abruptly.

"How are you doing with that?"

"How's any man going to take it if his wife kicks him out the door? Not too well."

Kevin's anger jumped out at me, and I found myself wondering how I was going to establish rapport with him. His rigid posture and pursed lips showed that he was not excited about being in my office and that just below the surface, he was in a lot of pain.

"Why did she ask you to leave?" I asked.

"You'd have to ask her. Something about me being no fun to be with anymore. She says I take things too seriously and let too many things get to me."

"Do you think that's true?" I asked, imagining his wife dealing with his attitude on a daily basis.

"I haven't been happy with my job the past few years. Lots

of politics at the mill, and they work me hard. I take some of my frustrations home with me. But is that enough for her to break our marriage vows?"

"Has she filed for divorce?"

"No, but she's threatened," he said. "And that's not something you do with me. That's not the Christian thing to do."

"Let's see if we can learn something from this situation. Maybe we can find a way to pull this thing out of the fire. Is she talking to you at all?"

"She'll talk to me as long as I promise to get some help and figure out what's bothering me."

"So why don't we do that?" I said. "Let's peel back some layers and see what this is all about. I know that I get irritable when I've got frustrations packed on top of frustrations. Is that possibly the case with you?"

"No doubt," he said. "I'm pretty mad at my boss, and the administration frustrates the daylights out of me. I'm the best millwright at the place, but I get no respect. I don't have any problems with the work—it's the politics that drive me crazy."

"Kind of like *Groundhog Day* at the mill, hearing the same negative messages again and again?" I said, trying to ease the tension a little.

"That's a good description."

"I'm curious, Kevin," I said, "is your wife willing to come in to see me too?"

"She mentioned that she was willing. I don't think she's throwing in the towel. She just wants me to be nicer when I walk in the door at night. She wants me to stop complaining so much and yelling. I guess I can't blame her."

"You know, Kevin," I said, "it sounds to me like if we get to the bottom of your frustration and find better ways of expressing it, you're going to have a wife again."

"That'd be nice," he said, offering a smile. "It's been mighty lonely around my tiny apartment, with the kids having left the nest and now her being gone. I'm not very good company for myself."

"And how's your faith?"

"I've been meeting with the guys at the church on Friday mornings, and that's helped a bunch. Don't know what I'd do without them. They've been praying for Lorene and me, and that's been great."

We spent the next few sessions delving into Kevin's history. He told me that he felt picked on at work by his boss, though he hadn't shared these frustrations with his wife. I saw that he was a quiet man, prone to internalizing problems rather than finding healthy ways to express emotions. He acknowledged that he had grown increasingly ill-tempered and possibly depressed over the past few years, and this had led to increasing conflict with his wife of 25 years.

Not surprisingly, Kevin had little understanding of his emotional life. He could barely differentiate his emotions and seemed surprised when I suggested he had many feelings that he needed to embrace, understand, and express. We explored his feelings of being hurt and rejected by his boss, abandoned by his wife, and tied in knots about the future of his marriage. He admitted that his negative attitude had pushed his wife away, yet he felt powerless to change his actions. He had known for months that his marriage was in jeopardy but tried to deny it, projecting blame onto his wife, which only increased the problem. He finally seemed ready to own his problems and admit that he needed to make some significant changes.

Specific Change Strategies

Kevin has a lot of work to do. As you may have noticed, his frustration is only one part of the problem. He has many destructive behaviors and thought patterns, but he doesn't know how to deal with them. Kevin's wife, Lorene, later shared with me that the dark attitude that came in the door with him wasn't the only problem. He had other issues as well. Lorene listed the changes she wanted to see him make, which greatly helped our counseling:

- take responsibility for his problems rather than blame his foul moods on others, including her

- stop generalizing—exaggerating her behavior with words like "always" and "never"

- tell her how he felt when she behaved in ways that bothered him, and ask for exactly what he needed

- stop setting himself up for frustration by expecting others to change their behaviors

- start learning ways to calm himself and explore ways of being happy

- allow her to view their world differently and have feelings and attitudes different from his

- learn to speak for himself and not for her, allowing her to make her own decisions

Kevin was defensive when he first saw her list of concerns, but he reluctantly admitted that they were valid. He came to realize that his distorted thinking had caused him to feel frustrated and irritable. Kevin learned some powerful tools in counseling and began to change his life.

Kevin started to grow emotionally by learning to focus on himself rather than on others. He took responsibility for his moods, admitting that they impacted everyone he came in contact with. He recognized that he needed to make changes in his life so he could be happy and then bring that happiness into his home. He learned to anticipate feeling frustrated and irritable and to recognize these emotions as warning signs that could teach him important lessons about himself. He discovered ways to calm himself down and to change his attitude so he didn't feed his aggravation. Together, we mapped out a multilayered strategy to help Kevin.

He would need to work hard in counseling if he was to save his marriage. He had been given a wake-up call that if things didn't change, his marriage would be over. He could choose how he wanted to proceed, and he discovered that he was very motivated to save his relationship with Lorene.

He would need to learn how to embrace and understand his feelings and make healthy emotional decisions based on them. Kevin needed to learn some basic emotional skills, such as understanding his feelings and learning to make good decisions based on those feelings. We discussed the importance of looking below the surface of his irritability, exploring other feelings that gave rise to the negativity and annoyance.

He would need to learn healthy self-care. He could not continue to bring his frustrations through the door with him every night. We noted that being tired and irritable occasionally was appropriate, but that he also needed to be pleasant and supportive to his wife most of the time. To accomplish this, he would need to deal effectively with his underlying problems and also learn self-care strategies such as proper exercise, nutrition, and sleep habits.

Finally, he needed to surrender his life to the care and wisdom of God. Rather than attempting to solve his problems independently, he needed to seek godly wisdom through his men's group, Bible reading, and prayer.

Kevin is still not back in the home, though his wife seems pleased with his progress. He struggles to embrace and understand his emotions, and most importantly, to take proper care of himself so he can be good company to his wife. Lorene expects even more changes, which at times irritates Kevin further.

Changing Our Thinking

The way we view the world largely determines the way we feel. If we modify our thinking, bringing it into alignment with sound scriptural principles and practical psychological tools, we will feel much less frustration and irritability. This is exciting news.

Let's consider what the Scriptures say about our thinking and the impact it has on emotions like dissatisfaction and irascibility.

The apostle Paul seemed able to handle the most frustrating circumstances with aplomb. How did he do it? Undoubtedly, one of his greatest resources was the Holy Spirit, whom he allowed to permeate his life.

"Do not conform any longer to the pattern of this world," he said, "but be transformed by the renewing of your mind. Then you will be able to test and approve what God's will is—his good, pleasing and perfect will" (Romans 12:2). We are to be in the continual process of transforming our mind. When the world says we should be frustrated that things don't go our way, the Word of God says, "Count it all joy when you fall into various trials" (James 1:1 NKJV).

Instead of getting angry when things don't go as planned and believing we deserve things to work out the way we want, we need to expect that life will deliver its share of disappointments. The Scriptures state that we will suffer in this life, and in fact, the Lord allows adversity to come into our lives. God's Word says, "No discipline seems pleasant at the time, but painful. Later on, however, it produces a harvest of righteousness and peace for those who have been trained by it" (Hebrews 12:11).

Society suggests we should take all we can get and get all we can take. We commonly believe we actually own what we have worked hard for, rather than seeing it as a gift from God and being stewards of these blessings. When we take ownership of our belongings and insist that we deserve them, we get bent out of shape when we don't get our fair share—and a little more. But the Scriptures tell us, "A generous man will prosper; he who refreshes others will himself be refreshed" (Proverbs 11:25).

General opinion seems to support taking revenge on anyone who stands in our way. We should hurt those who hurt us, fight those who fight us, get revenge on those who take things from us. After all, the world is our oyster and exists for our gratification, right? Once again, the Scriptures offer a better way. We are required "to act justly and to love mercy and to walk humbly with your God" (Micah 6:8). We are to be merciful even to those to whom we'd rather not show mercy. We are to walk and live with humility, serving others.

Fiercely grasping these worldly beliefs would be more understandable if they were productive and led to a peaceful life. But that's not the case. These worldly attitudes only create more frustration, estrangement from others, and isolation from God.

This quote, attributed to Jim Elliot, has had a powerful impact on my life: "He is no fool who gives what he cannot keep to gain what he cannot lose." When I consider my choices in light of this saying, I am humbled.

Leapfrogging Frustration

When I consider my adherence to scriptural mandates for my thinking and my behavior, I come up short. I repeatedly allow the world to get to me. I take things too seriously and resent disruptions that get in the way of my goals. I feel like a ten-year-old, wanting what I want when I want it, with no patience for anything that might interfere. But that's not the way things work.

Life *is* frustrating. People and events *do* get in the way of our intended goals. Just two days ago I had an experience that illustrated this point.

After another long day of counseling, I picked up a fresh salad and headed for the gym. I would have a rewarding workout and then a leisurely evening at home with Christie.

About 15 minutes later, however, I was following a large truck—a Ford F-350 to be exact—that entered an intersection and then stopped abruptly. I didn't, and in a moment, David met Goliath, except this time Goliath came out the victor. My new Beetle was scrunched under the big Ford, which came away with only a scrape.

Here was a golden opportunity to manage my anger—but I failed.

"I'm so glad you're safe," Christie said when I called her.

"But my car is wrecked, and it's my fault because I was following too closely. I could have avoided the whole thing if I'd been more careful."

"The car can be replaced. I'm just glad you're all right."

I spent much of my evening fuming as I talked to insurance companies and arranged for transportation to work the next day.

Here again was an opportunity—a gift. Here was a chance to practice the principles I share with my clients, such as learning to expect and accept hardship, tolerating frustrations, believing in the opportunity to gain from such experiences, acknowledging that I'm not in control of everything, and admitting that I don't have to have everything go my way.

After the dust settled, I lay in bed contemplating the evening. I thought of what John Lennon said: "Life is what happens when you're making other plans." Or, as someone else noted, "We make plans, and God laughs."

I'd like to learn to leapfrog my aggravation. Wouldn't it be great if we could feel annoyance and recognize that we're taking something, or ourselves, far too seriously? Wouldn't it be great if, when we felt irritability and frustration, instead of trying to control the situation, we could sit back in a moment of contemplation and get a clearer perspective?

Irritability and frustration are gifts, and they provide excellent opportunities to consider some other very useful tools, including acceptance, patience, and tolerance. The crises that enter our lives are opportunities to examine our thinking and stack it against the Scriptures, revealing the attitudes that cause us problems. For example, do you believe statements like these?

- *I can't stand this situation.*
- *This shouldn't be happening to me.*
- *I can't live without that person.*

Or do you believe these truths?

- *This situation will teach me something.*
- *I can tolerate this even though it's uncomfortable.*
- *I can sit with this hurt, and it won't overwhelm me.*
- *My painful feelings will subside—they always do.*

We can avoid much of our aggravation and bad temper. In fact, I think we can leapfrog a great deal of our emotional dissatisfaction. We do this by developing the mind of Christ and keeping things in an eternal perspective. With a spiritual maturity we see that things are only on loan to us, and troubles will come to teach us lessons.

I don't know if my car crash was ordained. More likely, it was a result of my own negligence. However, I do well to remember this Scripture:

> In this you greatly rejoice, though now for a little while you may have had to suffer grief in all kinds of trials. These have come so that your faith—of greater worth than gold, which perishes even though refined by fire—may be proved genuine and may result in praise, glory and honor when Jesus Christ is revealed (1 Peter 1:6-7).

My new goal is this: to learn from every stress and struggle that comes my way. The trials are inevitable—some suffering appears to be optional.

6

Anger: The Power to Change or Destroy

The world needs anger. The world often continues to allow evil because it isn't angry enough.

BEDE JARRETT

On a recent trip to Hawaii, my wife and I were amazed to witness the raw power of the volcanoes. Hawaii is one of only a few places on earth where one can view this energy close-up. Watching the molten lava ooze from the craters of Mauna Loa and Kilauea, we were awed and apprehensive. This level of energy cannot be completely comprehended or contained.

We approached Mauna Loa and Kilauea with wonder, excitement, and trepidation. When the lava reached the ocean, it spit and sputtered. This was primordial beauty, but it was dangerous as well.

A year earlier, Christie and I had traveled near the site of Mount Vesuvius. When that volcano erupted on August 24, AD 79, it devastated the city of Pompeii, killing thousands. Vesuvius also erupted in 1039, again killing thousands, and once more in 1631, killing another 4000 people.

Today, this same volcanic power is now being used for positive change. Hot liquid, buried beneath the mountain, is brought to the surface, where its steam turns turbines, creating electricity for area residents. The same power that killed so many now generates geothermal energy.

Like volcanoes, anger has the power to destroy and to heal. It is critical to making healthy decisions. Like irritability, anger is an instructive gift, able to teach us many things about ourselves. In this chapter, we'll learn how to manage this emotion, learn what it is telling us, and determine how to use it to make healthy decisions in our lives.

Hot Anger

Although anger can be incredibly instructive, it can be frightening and destructive as well. When we are angry, our muscles tighten, our pupils constrict, and our breathing becomes shallow, as we ready ourselves for combat. Adrenaline pulses through our bodies just as lava pulses through the depths of the earth beneath Mauna Loa and Kilauea. We use many phrases that picture the similarities between anger and volcanic power:

- explosive temper
- hot as a firecracker
- letting off steam
- spewing venom
- bursting with anger
- anger like a stick of dynamite
- a fiery temper

Most of us have seen or heard someone belching out expletives the way Vesuvius spewed out lava. We have been in the company of people who could not or would not manage their emotions. We've been frightened and hurt by their wrath.

I grew up with a stern and sometimes angry father. He wasn't always irritated, and I wasn't always frightened of him. But he was angry often enough to concern me. Even a small explosion goes a long way in announcing that an eruption is forthcoming with destructive consequences.

I can still picture my father coming into the house after a long day at the office and finding dishes in the sink and chores undone. With fire in his eyes, he muttered something to my mother, who was busy grading papers she'd brought home from her teaching job, and then started slamming kitchen cupboards.

Consumed by his tirade, he shouted not only at my mother but also at my younger sisters.

"What have you been doing all afternoon? I told you to have those dishes in the sink cleaned when I got home!"

And then he turned to me.

"Why haven't you taken out the garbage, David?"

I'd sputter something, having no good excuse. "I'll do it, Dad."

"Do it now!"

The unpredictability of my father's eruptions was the most confusing part. Generally a happy and even playful man, his anger frightened me. When I sensed he was in a foul mood, ready to pounce on someone, I'd head for the basement to hide out. I didn't like his anger and most certainly didn't like to be the recipient of it.

We were all frightened by my father's fiery temper, but at the same time we were told not to be angry with one another. What kind of advice was this? He was angrily telling us not to be angry. Or, as it was sanitized for us, "Do as I say, not as I do." This is the height of crazy-making. I tried to integrate his message, but it didn't work. It couldn't work.

Like Father, like Son

You'd think that with this history, I'd steer clear of the emotion. I haven't. Dad's motto of doing what he said and not what he did has failed to serve me well.

I entered adolescence like a runaway freight train with a locomotive of anger. I wasn't just angry—I was livid.

My rage, of course, was directed mostly at my father. When puberty hit, so did my sense that his anger and dictatorial control did not apply to my life. No longer confused or frightened by my father's anger, I wanted to knock the chip off his shoulder. I failed to see that the chip was primarily on my shoulder.

Over the next three years, my father and I fought about anything and everything. His obsession with the garbage now became the perfect opportunity for me to play him like a fiddle. I'd "forget" to take out the garbage and then dally even after he instructed me to get it done. He frequently lectured me about how I should treat my sisters with respect, get my hair cut, and work hard to improve my grades. Not surprisingly, none of his advice found a happy home.

My anger relented slightly following one last, grand eruption after I graduated from high school. I don't recall the issue, but something my parents said infuriated me. I burst into a rage, punched a hole in the living room wall, and stormed out of the house in defiance. My overt anger and explosiveness embarrassed and frightened me. I was acting in the very ways I disliked in my father. For a short season, I vowed to let go of anger.

Unfortunately, determination wasn't enough to extinguish the fire in my belly. My anger didn't readily subside, even after leaving home. I'd love to say that after I reached manhood, my emotional life made the transition to adulthood as well. It didn't happen. I grew in stature and earned several college degrees, but I didn't grow up emotionally.

I recall many times when I have erupted the same way my father had done. When something happened that I thought shouldn't happen in The World According to David, I'd go off, spewing venom at my wife and sons. When my sons were young, and later when they entered adolescence, a battle of wills ensued. I wasn't going to lose. Strangely, I felt that I had traversed this hostile land before—with my father 30 years earlier. I'm embarrassed to admit that I've exploded on my sons in ways that I deeply regret.

I have taken a great deal of time and patience to discover that I learned much of my anger from my father. I've also come to realize that I've disguised more sensitive emotions with anger. I've resorted to anger because I've not wanted to share my hurt, and I've worked in personal counseling and in many men's groups to resolve these issues.

Ambivalence About Anger

Having watched my father fall victim to his rage and then having replicated his mistakes in spades, I should not be surprised to learn that I've been puzzled about the proper place of anger in our lives. This was compounded by the fact that the church I grew up in taught me about an angry, vengeful God. Part Old Testament Warrior and part wrathful Father, the God I knew was filled with antagonism.

I pictured God as an old, bearded man with a perpetual scowl. And I had learned that He enjoyed smiting people. I didn't know exactly what *smiting* was, but decided it was akin to "now you see 'em, now you don't." In anger, He wiped out entire armies. He had the power to zap thousands of people out of existence with the flick of a finger, which He did to the Assyrians at Jerusalem's door. As a result, I spent years quaking in fear that I might do something to anger Him.

My early images of God aren't entirely fabricated. Although the church has enlightened me regarding the wonderful grace and love of God, I'm reminded occasionally that I must respect Him and consider His wrath.

A rereading of the Ten Commandments reminded me of these powerful words: "I, the LORD your God, am a jealous God, punishing the children for the sin of the fathers to the third and fourth generation of those who hate me..." (Exodus 20:5). Fortunately, the verse doesn't stop there but goes on to say, "...but showing love to a thousand [generations] of those who love me and keep my commandments."

I now see God not as an angry God, but a just God. The prophet Ezekiel says, "Because I tried to cleanse you but you would not be cleansed from your impurity, you will not be clean again until my wrath against you has subsided" (Ezekiel 24:13).

The Old Testament chronicles God's desire for a pure and holy people, blessing them when they were obedient and chastising them when they were rebellious. I've sometimes recoiled when reading of God's wrath, but it was always understandable and for the purpose of purifying His people.

The New Testament makes it clear that anger is a healthy emotion but that we must use it without sinning. "In your anger do not sin" (Ephesians 4:26, quoting Psalm 4:4). This is a helpful Scripture, assuring us that the emotion of anger is healthy but that the expression of anger needs boundaries.

The Scriptures provide more explanation:

- "Do not let the sun go down while you are still angry" (Ephesians 4:26).

- "But now you must rid yourselves of all such things as these: anger, rage, malice, slander and filthy language from your lips" (Colossians 3:8).

- "He who guards his lips guards his life, but he who speaks rashly will come to ruin" (Proverbs 13:3).

- "A patient man has great understandings, but a quick-tempered man displays folly" (Proverbs 14:29).

- "Better to live on a corner of the roof than share a house with a quarrelsome wife" (Proverbs 21:9).

Scripture appears fairly clear—we must respect, tame, and control our anger and never use it for destruction. This is a tall order, however, for an emotion that runs hot.

The field of psychology has added to our misunderstanding. Many of us have heard the importance of expressing this emotion and the destructiveness of "bottling up emotions." My doctoral dissertation, in fact, examined the suppression of anger and its impact in elevating blood pressure. These results have been replicated many times, as Jon Kabat-Zinn explains in his book *Full Catastrophe Living*:

> There is evidence that suppressing emotional expression may play a role in hypertension as well as cancer. In this area the focus has been primarily on anger. People who habitually express anger when provoked by others have lower average blood pressures than people who habitually suppress such feelings.[1]

The picture is hazy at best. Are we to express our anger or restrain it? How can anger help us make healthy decisions? The answer lies in our ability to live out what the apostle Paul said to the people in Ephesus—allow yourself to feel angry, but do not use your anger as a weapon of violence against others.

The Destructive Power of Anger

All emotion is helpful and natural, but anger can lead us astray in a heartbeat. The Scriptures are right to warn us of the many dangers of rage. Most of us don't spend time understanding and mastering this emotion, so we find ourselves suffering the nasty consequences of unbridled anger. Consider how many of us resort to one or more of the following immature expressions of anger:

- sarcasm
- passive-aggressive behavior
- physical explosions
- verbal tirades
- name-calling
- sulking

Most of us exhibit not just one but many of these forms of anger. Is it any wonder that our relationships suffer?

Dr. Harville Hendrix, in his popular book *Getting the Love You Want,* notes that he has witnessed the corrosive impact of anger. "Anger is destructive to a relationship, no matter what its form. When anger is expressed, the person on the receiving end of the attack feels brutalized, whether or not there has been any physical violence."[2]

I have seen these words ring true time and again in my work with couples. Those who insist on spewing their antagonism indiscriminately do irreparable harm to their marriage. A home filled with anger has no peace. When couples choose to unleash their fury on their mate whenever desired, they will never feel safe. Without safety and clear boundaries around the expression of anger, intimacy is impossible.

For years, counselors encouraged people to express their feelings, but we're now witnessing a change of opinion. The latest information tells us that unloading everything you feel on your mate is terribly destructive. Feeling an emotion and expressing it immediately, without consideration for your spouse, does not help build a healthy marriage or healthy individual lives. Impulsive actions are immature actions. The Scriptures counsel us to "take captive every thought" (2 Corinthians 10:5), and this includes angry thoughts.

Not surprisingly, Dr. Hendrix is just as opposed to repressed anger. "Whereas overt forms of rage create instantaneous damage, repressed anger often creates an empty marriage."[3] Hendrix says that repressed anger was the primary culprit in his depression and that unexpressed anger was a major reason for the dissolution of his first marriage. He tells us that being cut off from part of his being made him feel less than alive.

Many people struggle to find this balance between the expression and repression of anger. Some explode while others wallow in passivity, vowing that they will never allow themselves to feel rage.

We should not be surprised that Jesus illustrated the perfect balance. We see Him meek as a lamb and strong as a lion. He never pushed His own agenda but fully followed the plans of His heavenly Father. Those of us with confusing pictures of manhood can look to Jesus as a model of human behavior. Willing to make the difficult decisions of a leader, He also was willing to compassionately listen, poignantly share tears, and joyously celebrate with His friends.

Embracing Your Anger

With anger possessing so much potential for destruction, we are tempted to either suppress it or simply deny its explosive power. The trick is to find a balance between the two by embracing this powerful emotion. We must remind ourselves that anger itself is not destructive—violence is destructive. When one wants to harm another, that is not anger—that is violence. One has a right to be emotionally angry with others but not to behave violently.

Like other emotions, anger can be a gift that we must unwrap and explore.

First, anger can reveal what is important to us. Anger is an alarm that is set off when we feel violated. It signals that our boundaries have been transgressed in some way.

When we take the time to explore our anger, we learn about our core values. We learn the importance of trust, honesty, safety, and respect. Our anger reveals these truths to us, helping us define our identity. Anger has a positive purpose. It sends us messages, letting us know when our well-being or safety is threatened. Perhaps we feel manipulated or that our boundaries are being ignored. Anger is a signal that something is happening that violates our principles, boundaries, or sense of worth.

Second, anger can give us the power to make difficult decisions and carry them through. When faced with a challenge, we often need more energy, and anger gives that to us. The "fire in our belly" is steam that turns the decision-making turbines, leading us to action.

Third, anger defines our boundaries to others. Anger is a strong emotion that clarifies our firmness. We tend to respect those who respect themselves. We also teach people how to treat us, and our anger shores up our boundaries, sending a clear message to others.

Fourth, anger can be used to make important contact with others. In every relationship, anger can sometimes clear the air. As long as we still speak and act lovingly and remember that anger doesn't negate our goodwill for the other, anger can be an emotional point of contact.

Fifth, anger is a call to action. Although we never need to impulsively respond to a situation, anger tells us that we need to carefully consider what to do. We have a choice—and we can use this potent emotion to work for our good, to change circumstances and clarify our values. To do this, however, we must embrace this emotion.

Anger as a Way of Life

Sadly, many people have settled into anger as a way of life. You know the type—they fight against everything. They are angry at the government for taxes and foreign policy, they are angry at their neighbors for encroachments of various kinds, they are very angry at their parents for all the foibles and faults they lived under for years, they are angry at the pastor for preaching too forcefully, they are angry with their boss for a lack of respect, they are angry with their mate for any number of perceived transgressions, and underneath it all, they are angry with themselves.

Their lives are consumed by anger.

People who live in anger often embrace an attitude of entitlement, the belief that we should be able to have what we want, when we want it. As James wrote in his New Testament letter, "What causes fights and quarrels among you? Don't they come from your desires that battle within you? You want something, but don't get it" (James 4:1).

Isn't that the truth? Anger is often our immediate reaction when things don't go our way. However, this reaction is immature and almost always destructive.

People who live angrily are demanding. They seem to be saying, "I demand that things go my way," or "I demand that you obey me."

You know when you're around these people because their anger is ubiquitous and amorphous. They have a sense of entitlement and play the role of the victim deftly. They are complainers. They don't take responsibility for their lives, preferring to blame others for their problems. They let you know that if they had one break, any break, life would be much better for them. They embody anger.

People who are always angry get a huge secondary gain. They don't use anger as a tool to learn about themselves or as a warning sign that something may be wrong in their lives. They certainly don't take a deeper look to see if their anger hides other emotions. They actually enjoy being angry. They use their antagonism to bully, intimidate, and manipulate others—to gain power over those around them.

Notice the proliferation of road rage. The road warrior yells and gestures at other motorists, insisting that they drive better, faster, slower, or different. He acts as if he's become commander in chief of the highway, and things *will* proceed as he wishes, or he'll become enraged and seek vengeance against the transgressors.

Sitting back and taking note of this behavior reveals the issue for what it is—childish immaturity. It is ludicrous to think we can demand that someone speed up, slow down, use their blinkers, or drive in a different way. In fact, it is ludicrous to believe we can control others' behavior at all.

What Anger Hides

This kind of pervasive, enveloping antagonism is not useful. When we allow anger to fill us, rather than using it as a current for positive change, we must be alert to the possibility that something else is going on.

In my counseling practice, I see people who are accustomed to externalizing their fury. They cannot contain their anger and must project it immediately. They cannot "sit with" their anger and learn from it. These people must externalize their impulses immediately.

Most counselors believe anger is a secondary emotion. Hidden just below the surface are other emotions, such as hurt, sadness, and fear. Because many people cannot tolerate these softer emotions, they prefer to feel anger instead. Of course, this is more often true of men than women, as women are more comfortable with their softer emotions.

I recently worked with a husband and wife who were incredibly angry. I knew they were irate before even greeting them. As I approached this twentysomething couple, I could feel the tension in the waiting room. Sitting as far apart as possible and avoiding eye contact, they greeted me stiffly.

Doug was short and muscular with a solemn demeanor. His body language shouted, "Don't come too close." My friendly overtures met with one-word responses. He spent his time studying me and my office as we prepared for the session.

Lara was equally cool. Neatly dressed in business slacks and jacket, she appeared unhappy, with pursed lips and furrowed brows.

"So you guys have never been to counseling before?" I asked when we got started.

"Nope," Doug said. "Never thought I'd be in a shrink's office. But it is what it is."

"How about you, Lara?"

"No," she said. "I never thought I'd be here."

"Well, the best place to begin," I said, "is to tell me what's not working and what you'd like to change."

After this brief introduction, Lara and Doug launched into their issues. Before I knew it, they were firing bullets at one other. Doug blamed Lara for withholding affection from him, while Lara told him that his anger was intolerable. He told her he wouldn't be angry if she didn't overdraft their checking account, while she accused him of trying to control the money.

"Whoa!" I said almost immediately. "Where's all this anger coming from? Do you two argue like this at home?"

"This is nothing," Doug said sharply. "We're just getting started. She's a hotheaded blonde, and I'm Italian. Guess where that takes us?"

"It's going to take us to divorce court," Lara chimed in.

"Look, Doc," Doug said. "This is nonsense. She knows what she's done is wrong, and I shouldn't even have to talk about it. It's craziness. I shouldn't need to convince her not to overspend. But try telling her that. So we shout at each other and then don't talk for a couple of days until we both cool down."

"Do you think your anger is going to get you what you want in this relationship?" I asked.

"I never really thought about it," Doug said. "I've been this way for years. Same with her. It's all we know. I suppose there must be a better way."

"Yes," I said. "But you'll both have to want to learn that better way."

Lara and Doug were like couples I talked about in my book *Nine Critical Mistakes Most Couples* Make—they made the error of "pushing the emotional plunger." Without boundaries, couples like Doug and Lara let loose whenever they're upset. This causes rampant destruction, ultimately leading to the demise of the relationship if the problem is not corrected.

Dr. Hendrix adds, "If we repress our anger, we become sick or depressed or condemned to a pale, muted existence. But, on the other hand, if we unleash our rage, we inflict physical and emotional damage on others."

Our culture sees anger as powerful—volcanically strong. Society disdains other emotions as weak. These perceptions are erroneous. We don't have to squelch our anger—just manage it effectively. We don't have to deny our anger and the issues that touch it off, but we do have to contain it.

Dr. Hendrix offers a powerful tool for discovering the other emotions and issues that lie beneath our anger. The tool is aptly called *containment*. The exercise requires that each mate be the container for the other's angry emotions.

I encouraged Doug and Lara to practice this exercise. I taught them the importance of listening to each other's feelings without defending themselves. I encouraged them to listen for the real issue that needed to be addressed.

Doug began, with Lara listening and learning about his feelings. He shared his frustration and irritation about the checking account being overdrawn. He was able to admit being frightened about the condition of their finances. Lara listened to his feelings and validated his right to have them, although that was clearly difficult for her. Doug was not allowed to attack her character but only to discuss his feelings about her behavior.

When Doug was finished, Lara shared her feelings about feeling controlled financially. When he put her down, she felt inadequate and small. He was able to see how she might have these feelings.

With these boundaries providing safety, Doug and Lara were able to retrain their anger, stop attacking each other, and solve their problems. In this environment of acceptance, they could explore other feelings they might be having in addition to anger. Both expressed that they sometimes felt hurt and misunderstood. Although their surface emotion was anger, the container exercise encouraged each partner to explore other feelings below the surface.

As part of the containment exercise, I encouraged Doug and Lara to speak in "I" language, never pointing a finger of blame at each other. I also encouraged them to be on the lookout for other emotions. This took a great deal of practice because they were not familiar with anything but anger. Discovering other feelings allowed them room to more accurately note their inner experiences and to ask more specifically what they wanted from each other. These were powerful strategies in improving their relationship.

Healthy Anger

Anger is a normal emotion, and so it is neither good nor bad. What you do with it makes the difference. We've explored some of the ways we can use anger destructively. Now let's examine how we can use anger as a positive force for change.

First, make a conscious decision that you are going to manage your anger instead of letting it manage you. Determine to make constructive use of your anger rather than always having to apologize for expressing it in a destructive manner. Determine to explore the differences between righteous anger—focused on correcting some wrong in your life or the world—and selfish anger.

Second, develop a watchful attitude toward your anger. I call this *mindful living*. Instead of reacting impulsively to situations, practice noting what makes you angry and why. Place a pause button on your anger to give yourself time to understand why you might be reacting negatively to a particular situation. Solomon said, "A fool gives full vent to his anger, but a wise man keeps himself under control" (Proverbs 29:11).

Third, look below the surface to find underlying attitudes. Instead of rationalizing your anger—blaming it on the situation or another person—explore the possibility that beneath the surface lurks an attitude of selfishness or entitlement, or possibly other more vulnerable, unexpressed emotions, such as sadness, hurt, fear, or inadequacy. Ask God to enlighten you as you search for these attitudes and feelings.

Fourth, ask God to change your heart. As we are filled with the Holy Spirit, we break the habits of our fleshly nature. We cannot overcome our desires with our strength alone. We need the living water to quench the fires of our anger (John 7:38). Ask God for the courage to use your anger for positive change in the world and in your life.

Fifth, choose to use words that are encouraging and uplifting to others. As the apostle Paul said, "Do not let any unwholesome talk come out of your mouths, but only what is helpful for building others up according to their needs" (Ephesians 4:29).

Finally, ask God to change your selfish, immature thoughts. Ask God to purify your thinking so you become righteously angry only about things that need to be changed because they are wrong, not because you simply want things your way. Remember that God's ways are always higher than ours and that His thoughts are higher than our thoughts.

Anger can lead to destruction or to positive change. The choice is yours. The power within each of us can be volcanic, erupting at a moment's notice and leaving a path of destruction in its wake. Instead of settling for impulsive eruptions, however, slow down and take a look at the attitudes and beliefs that give rise to your reactions. By doing so, you will be prepared to make better choices for positive change in your life.

7

Resentment:
The Poison Pill

Holding onto anger, resentment and hurt,
only gives you tense muscles, a headache and a sore jaw
from clenching your teeth. Forgiveness gives you back
the laughter and the lightness in your life.

JOAN LUNDEN

Resentment has been called the poison pill. Ironically, we usually end up poisoning ourselves. The whole time we're hoping and wishing ill will come to those we resent, our toxic thoughts and feelings are eating us alive. The person for whom we harbor negative feelings may be completely oblivious to our feelings. After a while, we collapse emotionally and spiritually.

As I am writing this chapter, I am sitting by a pool at a bed-and-breakfast in a small town in Mexico. I am drawn again and again to this culture, which is marked by poverty, simplicity, and joy. The people here are friendly. The positive vibes flow freely and graciously.

The Mexican culture is known to be close-knit and full of mutual dependence and affection. The care and concern the people have for one another is legendary.

Out of curiosity, I asked an American expatriate innkeeper whether she agreed with my observation—that family and friends in Mexico seem to have very little resentment and hostility.

"They have so few possessions, but they're content with what they have," she said. "They don't begrudge one another what they do have and are always willing to help one another out. What is there to resent?"

"In the States we find plenty of things to resent," I said. "We resent someone for talking badly about us. We resent someone for overlooking us or intentionally hurting our feelings. We resent someone for not considering us when we think they should consider us. We resent someone who has more than we have or gets a job we had hoped for. We resent our siblings, our parents, neighbors, and even our friends."

The woman seemed incredulous. "Those same issues might arise in Mexico," she said, "but they wouldn't become problems. People wouldn't harbor grudges. They know they will work together the next day or will be with the others at a gathering soon, so they better not hold on to bad feelings."

"But those same things are true in the States," I said. "Even though we're going to be attending the same dinner in a few nights or worshipping at the same church, we hang on to resentments."

"I guess that's one of the reasons I was drawn to this culture," she said. "There are positive feelings everywhere. People laugh, share joys and sorrows, and create community. I'm not even sure there's a word for *resentment* in Spanish!"

"I hope someday we find some way to create this kind of love and acceptance in our communities. We're dying from the poison of resentment, creating and maintaining enemies nearly everywhere we turn."

Resentment Defined

I've asserted that emotions are not good or bad. The real issue is what we do with them. Resentment is unresolved anger left over from a negative event in our lives. It is anger we've allowed to stew until it reaches a point of emotional overload. By the time we resent people, we harbor animosity toward them and may wish that tragedy befall them.

Resentment, much like bitterness, begins innocently enough and then gains steam—a lot of steam. Resentment develops after we've made a decision, perhaps unconsciously, not to forgive someone for perceived wrongs done to us. Rather than work through our feelings of anger and hurt, we allow them to build into a cauldron of resentment.

Lest you feel like some kind of monster for having these feelings, remember that most of us have swallowed the poison pill at one time or another. Listen to gossip, and you'll hear how bad the boss is, how nasty the in-laws are, how insufferable parents are, and how ungrateful friends are.

These stories, usually exaggerated as time goes on, are told over and over again out loud and in the secret places of our mind. In fact, one definition of resentment is "angry and hurt feelings re-sent, again and again." Rehearsing our anger leads to resentment.

Clinging to Resentment

Why would anyone choose to cling to feelings of resentment? Resentment is the poison pill, but letting go of our pain is easier said than done.

Resentment is often the result of having been deeply wounded and perhaps victimized. We might sanctimoniously tell people they simply need to forgive but doing so is another story. Even though they are suffering from the memory of an emotional assault, letting it go can be an arduous task. Every wound creates myriad feelings that must be processed. Rarely is letting go of resentment a simple step.

Not long ago I worked with a woman whose husband of 40 years rejected her. Barbara was 60 years old and delightfully distinguished.

She carried herself with the grace and beauty of a princess. Her husband, however, no longer found her appealing and sought the interests of other women, and Barbara finally said enough was enough. Their marriage ended when he refused to stop his affairs.

Barbara struggles with a weighty load of resentment. She and her husband had prepared for the sharing of these later years—including having a vacation home in the sun and a healthy financial portfolio. She had worked some during their marriage, but he had been the primary breadwinner. Now, instead of enjoying the retirement she had dreamed of, she finds herself needing to work for several more years in order to be financially secure at a very minimal level.

Barbara bristles when talking about her ex-husband, refusing to even call him by name. "He" is the one who rejected her, abandoned her, failed to honor their marriage vows, slept around, and behaved so badly. She cries, hurts, yells, and rages. Her resentment has no bounds.

Does Barbara cling to resentment, or does resentment cling to her? Do we dare offer her platitudes about things being better in time or ask her to look at the ways she aggravates her situation? Can I encourage her to look into how she played a role in their marital demise?

Barbara's grief is immense—certainly too much for her to metabolize in a few sessions or a few months. She has been victimized by her husband's philandering. She must methodically process her anger and hurt. Even so, I believe what I've been saying throughout this book—her feelings will help her make important decisions. She can use her feelings to make positive change if she will allow this to play out.

Playing the Victim

I've worked with others who cling to and carry their resentments like badges of honor. For them, unlike Barbara, the problem is not so much a wound they cannot digest but almost a sense of pride about how badly they've been hurt. These people find some twisted pleasure in playing the victim.

Many who harbor resentment feel unjustly victimized, with no clear resolution in sight. I'm reminded of the mother of one of my clients. Sharon told me of her mother's suffering, the result of feeling victimized by a divorce from Sharon's father years ago.

"No one understands her," Sharon said. "Mom keeps talking about how Dad hurt her, but she won't move on with her life. She tries to get each of us kids to talk about him, but we don't want to do that. When we try to get her to let it go, she turns on us. She talks about us behind our backs, complaining that we don't appreciate everything she's done for us."

"What happens when you confront her about her feelings about your father?" I asked.

"She gets furious and then won't talk to me for a month. She tells my siblings what a lousy thing I did to her. It's always 'poor Mom,' and nothing is ever her fault. She wants to keep resenting Dad because that makes her the center of attention. And she doesn't mind resenting us either."

"It sounds like just being around her is draining."

"Are you kidding?" Sharon replied. "I can't stand to talk to her. Every conversation is an hour long, and she'll gossip about each of us, no matter how often I tell her to stop."

"Does she ever feel better?"

"No matter what we do, if we don't agree that it's all Dad's fault, she's angry with us. You'd think we never express any concern for her whatsoever. Nothing puts a dent in her resentment. She wants us to totally agree with her perceptions about Dad, but I don't agree with her."

"Is she really that upset with your father," I asked, "or are there other issues clouding the picture?"

"We all think it goes deeper than that. Her dad was an alcoholic, and Mom was really hurt by the way her parents treated her. Lots of rejection and pain from early in her life. But she won't talk about it. Instead, she focuses on Dad and us kids."

This appears to be an entirely different situation from Barbara's, who really was victimized. Sharon's mother clings to resentment as some perverted sense of identity. She must see herself as the rejected parent, the unloved one. Sadly, even offering her the very things she wants will not change her perception. She has viewed herself as the victim for so long that she cannot bear to live without that armor.

Those who act resentfully tend to create resentment around them. Can you imagine how difficult loving Sharon's mother would be? Her children are tired of her passive-aggressive maneuvers and other antics, and they have probably reached the point where they *do* reject her in some ways. She has succeeded in creating a self-fulfilling prophecy.

Signs of Unresolved Resentment

We all get angry sometimes, but being resentful means harboring bitter feelings and brooding over a perceived wrongdoing for an extended period. Resentful people usually don't realize how much this feeling poisons their lives. And they surely aren't using their emotions for positive change.

Barbara knew she resented her husband. She was fully aware that she also struggled with sorrow and loss. She knew that she wished bad things on her ex-husband and his current love interest. At the same time, she longed for the life she had known and the future she'd dreamed about.

Deep within Barbara's heart, however, things were beginning to loosen. In that small but growing space, she wanted to heal. She wanted to work through her resentful feelings and accept what had happened so she could move forward with her life. For that, I gave her a great deal of credit.

Sharon's mother, however, apparently didn't have a clue about how resentful she was. Each of her children could see *resentment* boldly tattooed on her forehead, but she disavowed being angry at all. Bitterness seeped out of every pore, yet she spoke as if she were Mother Teresa. How could she be so blind to this crippling resentment?

Sharon's mother is stuck. She becomes irritated if Sharon so much as mentions her father in a positive way. Sharon has tried to defend her father and siblings, but this has been futile because her mother chooses to cling tenaciously to her belief that she is getting a raw deal. She prefers to see herself as the victim and has no interest in doing her part to mend relationships. She doesn't want to embrace the possibility that she can move on with her life, and she won't try to envision a positive outcome for her difficult situation.

How can we know if we're more like Barbara or more like Sharon's mother? How can we determine if we have unfinished business in the resentment department? If we do these things, our inner emotions may be clamoring for some emotional decision making:

- feel irritable at the mention of a person's name
- stay away from a person to avoid angry feelings
- wish bad things for that person
- feel angry about that person's accomplishments
- sense an obvious barrier between us and that person
- talk about the person in sarcastic and angry tones
- reject all offers or suggestions concerning forgiveness
- resist moving forward with our lives

As you might suspect, resentment creates bad blood. Resentful people tend to be angry, irritable, and hard to like. Their brooding hostility has adverse effects on mood as well as physical well-being.

What is the impact spiritually? Resentment is sinful behavior, so clinging to bitterness creates a barrier between the resentful person and God. God is love and commands us to love others. Choosing to cling to resentment creates a chasm between the bitter person and God. The apostle Paul shares with us the appropriate attitude:

> Therefore, as God's chosen people, holy and dearly loved, clothe yourselves with compassion, kindness, humility, gentleness and patience. Bear with each other and forgive whatever grievances you may have against one another. Forgive as the Lord forgave you (Colossians 3:12-13).

As Christians, we have no room to linger in resentment. Our task is clear—let it go.

The Implicit Demands of Resentment

Letting go of resentment is much easier said than done. We must first be convinced that resentment is wrong. We must see resentment for what it is—a demand that others treat us the way we want and expect to be treated. We need to admit that we cannot control other people and that to demand that they treat us a certain way is ludicrous. We can only control ourselves.

Consider how foolish this conversation between Sharon and her mother would be:

"Sharon, I demand that you and your siblings share my belief about your father—that he did me wrong and that I was innocent in all of our problems. I insist that you all come running when I'm lonely. If you don't, I'm going to punish you by whining, being demanding, ignoring you, and gossiping about you and your father."

"Mom," Sharon might say, "you can ask us, and you can feel hurt if we don't respond the way you want, but it won't work to demand anything."

Not having a great deal of insight or mindfulness, Sharon's mom would likely come back with another inane comment. "Well, I believe everyone should see me as the victim and understand my right to cling to resentment. I reserve the right to be just as demanding as I want, and I demand that you see things my way. And believe me, if any of my children doesn't respond the way I want, I'll let her know about it in no uncertain terms."

"You can demand anything you want, Mom. But don't be surprised if we back away from you. It's no fun to be around someone who is resentful and demanding and then punishes us if we don't do exactly as they say."

For Sharon's mother, resentment is like bricks placed one on top of the other, walling others out and herself in. She is creating a very lonely existence.

Resentful people are demanding and irrational. They often believe the world is out to get them, that no one really loves or understands them, and that the people whom they resent have purposely done things to hurt them. This is rarely the case.

Beneath the resentment is this belief: *This shouldn't happen to me. I'm too important* (or good or smart or wealthy or loving or kind or...) *to have this happen to me. I'm above being treated this way.*

Rather silly, don't you think? When we examine resentment, we see a very childish attitude. Those of us who have harbored bitterness—and that certainly includes me—are like kids kicking sand in disgust. "No way!" we shout. "I won't put up with this!" And when we finally face reality, we discover that not only can we tolerate it, but we must.

The Gift of Resentment

Although we must accept the reality of certain negative behaviors, we are not obligated to allow those behaviors into our lives. This is where healthy boundaries come in. We control ourselves and can always walk away from abuse. We don't have to suffer in silence. In fact, we don't have to suffer at all.

Resentment, as with other emotions, offers a gift to us and a call to action. Let's consider some of the gifts of resentment.

First, resentment is a strong signal that you have unresolved hurt and anger. Rather than telling you something about the other person, resentment says a lot about you. It reveals a gaping wound that requires loving attention.

Second, resentment is a signal that you may be making unreasonable demands on others. As we've said, this is destined to fail because you can't truly demand anything of anyone. You can set limits on what you will tolerate, but not on what others might try to do to you.

Third, resentment points to a serious breach in a relationship, which creates an opportunity for reconciliation. This is a chance for God to transform your heart and perhaps to change the person you resent. It is an opportunity for God's grace to powerfully bring together two different points of view or heal a broken relationship.

Finally, resentment is an opportunity to better understand yourself. By looking at your wounds, you have an opportunity to understand what core value was transgressed. You can explore why you hurt so deeply and what you need in order to heal. You may have an opportunity to heal a wound from earlier in your life that has been reawakened by a recent incident.

Looking for the Deeper Wound

Emotions are signals that send us invaluable information. Even resentment, which is anger gone awry, carries opportunities for growth. Transformed resentment makes us more mature people with improved relationships.

Another gift of resentment is the opportunity to find the deeper wound many of us carry within. We naturally resist looking inside to uncover hurts and pain that we've long since buried. As with Sharon's mother, lingering resentment is often a signal that a severe wound needs attention. The focus of this deeper work is often not with the obvious symptom. The first step in releasing resentment is a willingness to explore, and that means being able to feel this deeper hurt.

Yes, remaining superficial is a tempting alternative. It is easier and less painful to look at others and say, "It's their fault. If it wasn't for them, I'd be fine."

Unfortunately, this is often not the truth. Even if it is, wallowing in resentment simply poisons our hearts and prevents us from living happy lives.

Might this current wound, this current resentment you carry and cling to, be a reminder of some previous anguish in your life? Chances are very good that this pain has been reawakened by the current issue.

Sharon's mother is a good example. Although she rails against her ex-husband, this rejection probably reawakened trauma she experienced earlier in her life. To her own detriment, she resists looking deeper and will probably never fully heal because of her denial and her tendency to blame others. She resists doing the necessary deep healing work.

Look beneath the resentment and find the true cause of the pain. Seek out those feelings you've been avoiding—of not being good enough or not feeling worthy of love. Then be willing to experience them. Cry if you can. Rage if you must. But take time to be with your pain. Allow the pain to rise to the surface where healing can occur. Once this has been done, you will find that you no longer need the resentment.

Forgiveness

We cannot talk about loosening the grip of resentment on our lives without talking about forgiveness, the tool God has given us for this very situation. However, this is a challenging area for most of us.

When I'm honest with myself, I realize that I often don't want to forgive those who have hurt me. In fact, I want to seek revenge. I want others to feel the pain I've felt.

But then I stop in my tracks.

The Scripture says, "And when you stand praying, if you hold anything against anyone, forgive him, so that your Father in heaven may forgive you your sins" (Mark 11:25). Ouch! Forgive others so that my heavenly Father may forgive me? But I don't want it to work that way. I want to receive unconditional forgiveness while granting only conditional forgiveness to others.

Forgiveness is a tall order. It doesn't come easily and often doesn't come under our own power. We naturally hold on to our pain and demand that others act in a different way to obtain our forgiveness. Here is where we truly need the power of the Holy Spirit to change our hearts, to bring love into every critical situation. Then we will be able to follow this scriptural injunction: "If your brother sins, rebuke him, and if he repents, forgive him. If he sins against you seven times in a day, and seven times comes back to you and says, 'I repent,' forgive him" (Luke 17:3-4).

Our first response is to protest. And then we're reminded of what Jesus did for us.

"My dear children, I write this to you so that you will not sin. But if anybody does sin, we have one who speaks to the Father in our defense—Jesus Christ, the Righteous One. He is the atoning sacrifice for our sins, and not only for ours but also for the sins of the whole world" (1 John 2:1-2).

Forgiveness says, "I release you from your debt to me. I no longer hold anything over your head. I won't keep rehearsing how you've wounded me—I'll let love into the spaces where I cling to resentment. You don't need to change or give me anything. I fully understand what Jesus has done for me, and I grant you what I have freely received."

Does forgiveness mean that we deny the pain we have received from the offender? Not at all. I don't think there is any way to short-circuit our pain. The only way to be rid of it is to go through it. Remember, a feeling denied is intensified. We must do our grief-related work, and we must do it thoroughly.

Forgiveness *does* mean that we consider what Jesus did for us and what we are told we must do for others who have offended us.

Dealing effectively with our anguish and allowing God to work in us will eventually melt away our resentment.

More Steps to Forgiveness

The path to forgiveness is never straight or simple. Forgiveness is never just an experience of the head—you must do heart work as well. We are rarely able to simply will ourselves into forgiving someone. It takes work. Here are a few suggestions:

- Identify who has hurt you and exactly what they did to make you resentful.

- Identify the precise thinking errors that may perpetuate your anger and resentment.

- Determine to let go of those thinking errors and to begin thinking in healthier ways.

- Once you've identified each person you resent and the extent to which this resentment has affected you, seek a new way of looking at your past, present, and future life.

- Expand your perception of the people you resent. See them in broader ways than right or wrong, good or bad. Realize that they are multifaceted people.

- Visualize your life free from the negative thoughts and attitudes that have perpetuated your resentment. Practice thinking in new ways toward the people you've resented.

Don't expect forgiveness to be easy. The extent to which we struggle with forgiveness may indicate the depth to which we've been hurt. The greater the wound, the longer we'll need to work to find forgiveness in our hearts.

Letting Go

Although Barbara's pain is deep and her resentment is great, she must learn to let it go. Her bitterness and other emotions are signals to her that she needs to take action. She cannot afford to linger with her resentment, rehearsing again and again the ways her ex hurt her, how she didn't deserve the life she got, or how she must now make difficult choices that she has no desire to make.

She must face her life today and consider her choices. Of course, this won't be easy.

Letting go for any of us means listening to our feelings and taking the time to examine the thoughts feeding those emotions. Barbara realized that her resentment indicated that she was rehearsing thoughts of being victimized and replaying her rage toward her ex-husband. She had worked hard to convince herself that she was getting a bad break, that she had nothing to do with her problems. Letting go of resentment meant looking at her life through new eyes. It includes actions like these:

- widening our point of view
- seeing our part in the problem
- seeing the offending person with new, loving eyes
- looking for the positive in the current situation
- not attributing horrible motives to the offender
- seeing the offending person as worthy of forgiveness and God's love
- grieving fully over our losses
- courageously moving forward with our lives
- trusting God to take care of us

Barbara prepared to change her life by moving from the Pacific Northwest to Southern California, where she had a number of close friends. She decided that this was the perfect opportunity to make a break between her old life and the possibilities of a new one.

Barbara also dove into the Scriptures to see what God might have for her. Her crisis provided the impetus for her to seek God in new ways. She shared with me that her prayer life had deepened and that she had found new strength and comfort in the psalms. Her spiritual life was invigorated.

Barbara decided to go back to work but took some time to decide what kind of job she wanted to do. She decided not to jump at the first thing that came along but rather to choose a job that would be fulfilling. She is excited about the possibilities.

Most importantly, Barbara is beginning to feel less pain and resentment toward her ex-husband. She is slowly exploring her part in their marital failure and the lessons she can take into a new relationship, should that possibility occur. She feels hopeful that she might someday have another chance at love. If so, she will make the most of it.

Koinonia

Once we understand the issue of resentment and its corrosive impact on our lives, we open ourselves to the possibility of a different life and different decisions. We invite the gift of resentment into our lives.

Of all the Scriptures, one stuns me more than the others. It is the picture given to us of the early church after it had received the Holy Spirit. Here is a description of a community of people living consciously without resentment. It is a community committed to partnership—to *koinonia*.

> All the believers were one in heart and mind. No one claimed that any of his possessions was his own, but they shared everything they had. With great power the apostles continued to testify to the resurrection of the Lord Jesus, and much grace was upon them all. There were no needy persons among them (Acts 4:32-34).

Consider the impact of this stirring passage. All believers were of one heart and mind. How is this possible? What happened to the factions? What about the squabbling and backbiting that naturally occurs when two or more are gathered? Even more incredibly, not only were there no factions or divisions, but everyone shared what they had with one another. No one needed anything!

The only way to understand this Scripture is to note an important clause: "Much grace was upon them all." Grace explains it all. Supernatural, unmerited favor covering all of them by the power of the Holy Spirit.

If we are to find power to heal our resentments, we must look to the Holy Spirit, the indwelling power of Jesus Christ in our lives. Left to our own devices, I'm afraid we'd muck things up pretty badly. But when we give ourselves over to the power of Christ, we change. We give up childish demands, petty squabbles, and the need for others to change in order for us to be happy. Acts 4:32 gives me hope that we actually can gather together without fighting or resentment. It *is* possible.

8

Depression: Anger Turned Inward

My heart pounds, my strength fails me;
even the light has gone from my eyes.

PSALM 38:10

Writing much of this book while on vacation in Mexico was a gift because it allowed me to leave behind the wet, gray winter of the Pacific Northwest. Feeling the pulsing life of sunny climates, alive with outdoor living, reminds me that seasons and situations evoke distinct moods.

Just as sure as there are verdant, green oases in Mexico and other tropical climates, other regions are dull and gray in the dead of winter. The deciduous trees have lost their foliage, leaving a monochromatic landscape. Even the clouds sulk with their burden of heavy rain or biting snow.

Winter's darkness and brooding silence remind me of depression—the inner expanse of deadness. Other "darker" emotions, such as anger, irritability, and bitterness, at least make us feel alive, but depression seems to be absent of any emotion. All we feel is numbness. Resentment and bitterness signal a disorder within that needs attention, but the numbness of depression too often leads to a series of dead ends. But like our other emotions, depression pulses with possibilities for positive change if we listen closely.

Although we wouldn't wish depression on anyone, valuable messages are available to us within even the most sullen mood. The darkest hour can be the most enlightening. Even a depressing state can be ripe for momentous change. It can lead to a powerful time of decision making if we embrace the emotions that accompany the depression.

Depression Defined

Depression is a very misunderstood disorder. It is often hidden because so few people step forward to admit that they've struggled with it. Thirty-five years ago, we determined that Thomas Eagleton was not fit to run as a candidate for vice president of the United States because he admitted that he struggled with depression. Sadly, we've not made much progress in understanding this condition.

Although depression is a common problem, most people don't want to talk about it, especially in Christian circles. We Christians have a tendency to focus on what we consider positive emotions, denying the presence of the more challenging ones. If we are daring enough to talk about the subject, the conversation will likely be about someone else's depression, not our own.

Generally, when we talk about depression, we are referring to an illness that involves the body, intellect, and emotions. It affects the way people eat and sleep, the way they feel about themselves, and the way they think.

Depressive disorders affect approximately 18.8 million American adults, or about 9.5 percent of the U.S. population age 18 and older. The primary types of depression include major depression, dysthymic disorder, and adjustment disorder with depressed mood. The difference between these conditions has to do with their length and severity.

A depressive disorder is not the same as a passing blue mood.

It is not a sign of personal weakness or a condition that someone can wish away. In fact, people usually cannot pray it away, as much as prayer may help the situation. People with a depressive illness cannot merely pull themselves together and get better. Without clinical intervention or significant spiritual, emotional, and lifestyle change, symptoms can last for weeks, months, or years. Thankfully, the condition is treatable in most cases.

Symptoms of Depression

Different mood disorders have different symptoms, but clinical depression, or the diagnosis of dysthymic disorder, is usually marked by the following symptoms:

- persistent sad, anxious, or empty mood
- feelings of hopelessness and pessimism
- feelings of guilt, worthlessness, and helplessness
- loss of interest or pleasure in hobbies and activities, including sex
- fatigue and decreased energy
- difficulty concentrating, remembering, and making decisions
- insomnia, early-morning awakening, or oversleeping
- appetite loss and accompanying weight decline or overeating and accompanying weight gain
- thoughts of death or suicide
- suicide attempts
- restlessness and irritability
- persistent physical symptoms, such as headaches, digestive disorders, and chronic pain, that do not respond to treatment

Depression includes problems with thoughts and behavior, but the primary area of concern is the emotions. Persistent sad and anxious moods as well as feelings of helplessness, loss, guilt, and pessimism are most common.

Tragically, one of the primary problems with depression is a feeling of emptiness or dullness. This renders people stuck, leading to passivity, which only aggravates the problem. Many depressed people talk about a fog that settles into their mind, making it particularly difficult for them to make decisions. Understandably, emotional decision making is a challenge when your mind seems to move like molasses.

Depressed people often have slowed thoughts and behavior, feel hopeless about the quality of their life, and then behave accordingly. This leads to a loss of interest in activities and a withdrawal from friends and family as the cycle continues. The mood worsens if sufferers don't tend to their symptoms of depression immediately and make corrective decisions.

Causes of Depression

Theories abound regarding the causes of depression. Rarely is there just one cause. These are some of the best-known causes of depression:

- genetic predisposition
- biochemical imbalance
- physiological difficulties, including exhaustion
- dysfunctional behavior patterns
- maladaptive thoughts
- self-destructive beliefs
- early life trauma

All of these can cause problems, but my experience suggests that troubled relationships with others, with one's self, or with God are often primary causal factors.

Bob Murray, in his book *Creating Optimism,* asserts that relationship problems are at the root of virtually every depression. He has also found childhood trauma and abuse in most people who succumb to serious depression. He suggests that childhood trauma results in serious problems with self-esteem and the effective management of feelings. He stresses the importance of identifying the negative beliefs and behaviors that keep you stuck in the past and that continue to trigger feelings of trauma. Murray suggests that a primary antidote for depression is competence.

> One of the main components of satisfaction in life is what is called "sense of competence." It's difficult to feel any lasting self-esteem without it…It is the knowledge that you do some things really well, such as raising your children to be happy and healthy people, painting exquisite watercolors of local scenes, making things that other people find beautiful or useful, or even perhaps heading a large corporation.[1]

How does any of this tie into our emotional life? Quite simply.

Embracing our feelings and tuning in to what brings us pleasure helps us find meaningful activities. This doesn't mean we involve ourselves in only hedonistic pleasures but that we find our *calling* in what delights us—what we were made to do. We then pursue meaningful activity in our work or as a volunteer. But we must be tuned in to our emotions to even know what brings us pleasure.

Losing sight of what brings us pleasure is one of the leading causes of depression. Having denied our feelings, we become numb, we suppress our anger and our joy, and soon we are like zombies going through the motions of life. Having tuned out uncomfortable feelings, the rest of our feelings turn numb as well.

But doesn't everyone naturally know what brings them pleasure? Do we really need to tune in to our feelings to know this? Actually, most young children know what brings them pleasure, but many adults lose sight of this basic ability. Adult responsibilities, the seriousness of life, and many shame-based messages about disregarding our feelings combine to send our childlike pleasures into the cellar of our soul. Recovering from depression requires us to dig into the roots of our soul, find our childlike nature, and rediscover what brings us delight.

"You don't have to be the world's greatest mother, watercolorist, or manager," Murray says, "to achieve a sense of competence; you just have to *feel* that you're good at what you do…Happiness depends on being able to do things that make you feel competent."[2]

Listening to our feelings is not a frivolous activity, but a primary responsibility. It keeps us healthy.

Denial of Feelings

When we deny our feelings, we are in peril. Our emotions are such an integral part of our nature that to deny them is to cut ourselves off from a central aspect of our being—as well as a critically important source of information. Don Baker and Emery Nester, in their book *Depression,* make this clear:

> If denial of feelings becomes part of a lifestyle, we leave ourselves vulnerable and exposed to the ravages of emotional illness. Feelings of anxiety and anger, when repressed or denied, will move us toward neurotic illness. Inability to adequately deal with these conditions causes less effective functioning. We become unable to deal with our inner lives and therefore less able to grow in genuine qualities of humanness.[3]

We might wonder if this explanation is too simplistic. Is denial of our feelings not only going to cut us off from a primary source and power of decision making but also lead to emotional illness? Yes. We know of other causes of depression, but denial of feelings is near the top of the list. Why? As Baker and Nester say, denial of feelings makes us lose touch with our inner lives. Feelings of anxiety and anger can help us make critical decisions.

Denial of feelings is a central problem in depression and many other emotional disorders. As psychologists assist their clients in excavating hidden feelings, we often focus our hunt on two: anger and anxiety—major culprits in creating depression. Many people are particularly uncomfortable with these two feelings and find ingenious ways to distance themselves from them. In doing so, they find momentary relief but long-term emotional problems.

Dark Moods

I came home from work recently, excited about the surprise trip I had planned to Mexico. When I walked through the front door, Christie hardly acknowledged my presence, something quite unusual for her. Working frenetically on a final assignment from school, she muttered a hello.

I could tell from her disposition that something wasn't quite right.

"Are you okay?" I asked.

"No," she said, sounding exasperated, "I'm not. You're going to have to get yourself something to eat. I'm stressed."

"What's up?" I asked.

"What's up?" she echoed. "Finals, laundry, cleaning, and getting ready for this trip."

Tiptoeing back into the discussion, I tried to offer her support.

"What can I do to help?" I asked.

"Well," she said, without looking up, "you can finish this project for my final. Then wash our clothes and pack. I think a better idea would be to leave me alone. I'm not very good company."

With that I left the room, wondering what was going on with my wife. I'd seen her stress mounting in recent weeks, to be sure. Her irritability had worsened, and she seemed to be losing her generally good nature. Something was different. I wondered if she could be depressed. Her mood had been worsening, her energy was waning, and her sleep was fitful—all signs of possible depression.

Christie and I had a long talk the next day. Although she was in a better mood after a good night's sleep, she still was not her usual positive self. She needed to reconsider the direction of her life. She felt overwhelmed with certain aspects of her life and wondered how she could balance everything on her plate. She definitely needed to review her lifestyle.

Most important, Christie needed to attend to her feelings, particularly anger and anxiety. She needed to feel the weight of her choices and decide whether to continue to attend school full-time while handling the responsibilities with our home and children. She also wanted to enjoy the recreational time we share together. Although she apologized for her foul mood and told me not to take it personally, she knew that these feelings were trying to tell her something important. She needed to listen to her dark mood to influence choices she'd have to make about her life.

Together, we decided that recent illnesses had left her more tired and irritable than usual. She still had some feelings of hopelessness, another symptom of depression. She was tired of attending college but still had two years to go in order to complete her interior-design degree. She was also nearing the end of her college quarter, when pressures are greatest. We agreed that though she might not be clinically depressed, she was susceptible, and we needed to be cautious. We agreed to reconsider some of our decisions about packing too much into our lives.

Christie's spirits bounced back fairly quickly during vacation. Lying by the pool, taking siestas, and eating well helped recoup her energy. We also used our vacation to talk about other challenges facing us during this upcoming quarter. She would be gone for long hours on some days, and we needed to prepare for this as a couple. I would need to listen carefully to her needs and assist her in the care and management of our home. We agreed that she needed to be tuned in to the presence of irritability, anxiety, and anger as precursors to possible depressive tendencies.

Exhaustion

Christie believes she was mildly depressed, and hidden beneath her depression were feelings of anxiety, anger, and apprehension. She was trying to do too much and was angry at herself for loading her plate too full. She was also tired and needed the vacation.

Many depressed people are exhausted, and they do not recognize or accept their underlying emotions. We live in a fast-paced world and burn the candle at both ends. We work too hard and forget to take time-outs to pull ourselves together again. We run and run until we collapse, failing to listen to our bodies or our emotions. Were we to listen more carefully, perhaps we'd live different lifestyles.

Again, I'm reminded of our trip to Mexico, and another, a year ago, to Spain. Both cultures are slower paced than ours. Both embrace the siesta, and shops and businesses close from one to four each afternoon. In many European cities, shop owners literally roll down their window screens at one o'clock, regardless of whether customers are in the store at the time. Siesta is for napping, chatting with friends, and mingling with family. This is sacred time.

In like manner, Sundays are sacred times in many cultures. Just as God rested after creating the world, the Jewish culture pays particularly close attention to keeping the Sabbath holy, sacred, and set apart. It is a time to rest and recuperate, putting aside daily worries and work. It is a time for the mind to regenerate, readying itself for the week ahead.

In observant Jewish homes, *Shabbat* begins each Friday night at sundown when a woman lights the Sabbath candles. It is a festive time; people dress up, use the best tableware, prepare the best food, and welcome guests. In some families, everyone faces the door and sings to greet *Shabbat*, which Jewish hymns personify as a loving bride who brings inner delight or as a beautiful queen who delivers order and peace. Traditional prayers give thanks; indeed, mourning is suspended in *Shabbat* liturgies. Many families sing or read together after the meal. They will gather again the next evening for another meal at which they will bid farewell to the holy day. Finally, parents bless their children and give them a bit of sweet spice so that the taste of Sabbath peace lingers on their tongues.

Jewish liturgy and law stipulate what should be done on *Shabbat* and what should not. The faithful should not work. Defining exactly what that means is a long and continuing argument, but one classic answer is that work is whatever requires changing the natural, material world. All week long, we wrestle with the world, tilling and hammering, carrying and burning, managing and constructing. On the Sabbath, however, Jews let it be. They celebrate the world as it is and live in peace and gratitude. By gratefully receiving the gift of the world, Jews acknowledge that human effort does not make the grain grow. That's why all activities associated with work or commerce are prohibited. Devoted Jews should not even think about them.

Our culture is definitely in danger of worshipping the almighty dollar and the gods of capitalism, consumerism, and work. We leave ourselves little time for rest, family, and spirituality. Americans work far more hours today than ever before, so the trend is not changing. This leaves us susceptible to overwhelming our immune systems as well as our emotional balance.

Elijah

Depression is often the result of an overwhelming event or longstanding task that we must face when our emotional reserves are depleted. Such was the case with Elijah.

Elijah had just completed one of the most dramatic episodes of his career. He'd routed the soldiers of evil King Ahab several times. He gathered the king, the people, soldiers, and four hundred false prophets in one location. Once there, he boldly challenged the prophets, and when they failed to call down fire from heaven to devour the sacrifice, the confident and powerful prophet Elijah called on God to send fire from heaven and consume the sacrifice. He then boldly ordered that the false prophets be executed.

A short time later, however, Elijah seems to become a changed man. We find him running for his life from Queen Jezebel, who vowed to kill him. Now Elijah, the man of faith, who had just called down fire from heaven, became filled with fear and ran as a coward to hide in the desert. Once there, he seems to fall into a situational depression.

This picture of Elijah is important for us to consider. Depression is usually a result of improper thinking that leads to unruly emotions or unhealthy decisions, but Elijah offers another perspective. Elijah seems to have succumbed to depression as a result of physical exhaustion.

Elijah had been in physically demanding situations for many years. He outran King Ahab's chariot after the rains came, and this had further drained his energies. Now, a victim of wavering faith and overwhelming fear, he runs and hides. His exhaustion caused his emotions to be out of balance, and then his depression led to further cloudiness in his thinking. In Elijah, we see an example of how quickly emotions can become unbalanced and lead to poor decision making.

Elijah was exhausted and frightened, and his emotions continued to tumble like dominoes. When one emotion seemed to pile onto another, his emotions became exaggerated. (The same thing happens to us.) He felt ashamed, angry, and even suicidal. He wearied under the weight of anger turned inward, anger turned outward, frustration, and fear. After all the great things he had done, he wanted to die. Ashamed at his failure and discouraged with his actions, he became so depressed, he was unable to do the basic things necessary to survive. He begged God to let him die.

But this wasn't in God's plans. Elijah didn't need to die, he didn't need long-term therapy, and he didn't need medications. He needed food and rest. He needed to sit back and obtain a new perspective. For this reason, God sent an angel to feed Elijah, give him water, and allow him to sleep.

I can relate to Elijah. Not that I've performed any miracles or reached any of the pinnacles he attained. But I've allowed pride to consume me. I've pushed myself to exhaustion and then wondered why I felt so discouraged and empty. In my tiredness I've learned, like Elijah, to listen carefully to God. In that quiet, I've sensed His leading in my life. I've learned about the exquisite interrelationship between our physical, spiritual, mental, and emotional well-being. I've learned that to make good decisions, I must not only listen to my emotions but also listen to my body.

Heeding the Warnings

Elijah's example can teach us several lessons. Although self-care might seem obvious, many of us don't listen to signals from our bodies, so we unwittingly increase our physical and emotional problems. If we abuse the vessels God has given us, we can expect some kind of breakdown. Fortunately, there are easy remedies.

Caring for our bodies is a spiritual responsibility. After all, our bodies are not our own—they belong to God. We are to be good stewards of them, making sure we eat properly, exercise, and rest.

A second warning from Elijah's life is that we should pause and take inventory when trouble arrives. Solomon said, "When times are good, be happy; but when times are bad, consider: God has made the one as well as the other" (Ecclesiastes 7:14). When trouble hits, we need to slow down, rest, and consider the best choice of action. We need to pay attention to our emotions and our thoughts and then carefully make the best decision possible.

Making a critical decision when we are emotionally reactive is almost always unwise. So is making a critical decision in the midst of fear. We need a clear mind and balanced emotions to make pragmatic decisions. We need time in prayer, where we can listen to the voice of

God. After praying, we need to carefully weigh our emotions, consult with friends, and then decide.

A third warning is to keep things in perspective. God is God, and we're not. We can't control circumstances. Elijah began to trust in his own resources rather than relying completely on God, who had brought him to the height of success. We are in danger of the same discouragement and depression when we believe things must turn out a certain way. When we rely on God, we trust that He will work for our best good. We make plans as He leads and encourages us, but we allow God to open and close doors as He desires.

Finally, a fourth warning from Elijah's life is to be cautious about making a decision in a time of crisis. We are almost always wiser simply to be still than to make a decision reactively. When our emotions are fluttering all over the place and our thoughts are bouncing around wildly, we should wait for a better time to make important decisions.

A little rest, some good food, and a change of scenery can be powerful decision-making tools. The world looks amazingly different when we feel healthy and rested.

A Message from the Soul

All of our trials, even depression and the emotions associated with it, can bring a helpful message to us. Thomas Moore sheds some light on this in his book *Care of the Soul:*

> Care of the soul doesn't mean wallowing in the symptom, but it does mean trying to learn from depression what qualities the soul needs. Even further, it attempts to weave those depressive qualities into the fabric of life— coldness, isolation, darkness, emptiness—and makes a contribution to the texture of everyday life.[4]

What might the soul be teaching us through our depression? What might be the gifts hidden in this dark period?

First, this is a time to slow down. After easing our pace because of sheer exhaustion, we have the opportunity to consider our plight. We cannot review our life when we're frenetic. Our problems require our complete focus.

Depression forces us to pull back, to stop what we've been doing. As in the dark days of winter, we are forced inside, and in this way, depression, despite its painfulness, can be instructive.

Second, depression forces us to look inward. We might not like our agitated condition, but it motivates us to reflect on our pain. Do we need to change a relationship? Do we need to alter our lifestyle in some way? In a season of distress, the psalmist wrote, "Oh, that I had wings like a dove! For then I would fly away and be at rest" (Psalm 55:6).

No one wants to feel depressed. However, this dark, quiet place and time can bring rich rewards. When we turn our energies outward, we tend to neglect our spirit. When we dash frenetically through life, we fail to pay attention to our inner emotional, intellectual, and spiritual life.

Third, depression can cause us to make necessary changes. Are you no longer content to stay in that bad job or suffer in an abusive relationship? Depression shouts at us to make adjustments. Perhaps depression tells us to lose weight, seek treatment for alcohol abuse, or get counseling. Depression forces us to try something different from what we've been doing.

Finally, depression often forces us to look to God for help. When we've reached the end of our rope and used up all our resources, we're forced to seek God's help. With our resources depleted, we feel compelled to seek higher advice.

Depression, for all of its pain, can be a messenger bearing gifts. It can be a way for the soul to scream out for our attention and make us ready to listen.

Helping Yourself

As with any significant problem, taking a proactive approach with depression will serve you well. Not surprisingly, passivity exacerbates the problem. If you wait for the depression to naturally lift or for life's circumstances to change, you may be waiting too long. One of the primary purposes of this book is to encourage you to become an expert at listening to your feelings, attending to your thoughts, and then making critical decisions. You can take advantage of several more practical strategies.

First, obtain a good medical workup. Depression has many causes, and some of them are medical. Even if your physician doesn't find any organic causes, he or she can determine if you have physiological symptoms—such as loss of appetite, fatigue, and sleep disturbance—that might suggest you're a good candidate for antidepressants.

Don't try to be a hero when it comes to medications. Just as a diabetic needs insulin, the depressed person may need some medical assistance to boost neurotransmitters in the brain. When brain chemistry has been altered by prolonged stress or depression, medications are usually a critical part of an effective solution.

Second, exercise. Exercise has been called the "fountain of youth" or "the great elixir of life." Exercise is associated with too many benefits to mention here, but there are a bunch. Exercise creates and releases some of those wonderful feel-good neurotransmitters (endorphins) in the brain, helps us think more clearly, makes us feel better, and yes, even helps us make better choices. You know the benefits of exercising, so if you haven't made it a ritual, "Just do it!"

Third, develop a healthy diet. Good nutrition can powerfully impact your decision-making prowess and your self-image. "You are what you eat" has more than a grain of truth in it. A diet rich in protein and complex carbohydrates will get you going and keep you going.

Fourth, fill your mind with good thoughts. Read and reflect on good self-help material (see my book *Does Your Man Have the Blues?*) and other readings you find beneficial. Familiarize yourself with material about depression. Additionally, fill your mind with spiritual food. Read the Word, finding special encouragement from the psalms during darker days.

Fifth, foster an optimistic attitude. Although this is certainly difficult when you're feeling down, you can make choices to think about good things. You can challenge your depressive thoughts, the ones telling you that things will never change, that you're worthless, and that there is no hope. You must develop another part of yourself that tells yourself the truth--that you can do many things to improve your life.

Count your blessings. Do you have material and financial blessings? Be thankful and generous with others. Visiting sick friends reminds us that we are fortunate to have our health. Are you happily married? Be thankful. Do you have family and friends? Be thankful. Count your blessings.

Finally, get in touch with your feelings, especially anger. We often experience relief when we finally feel our anger instead of suppressing and swallowing it. As Baker and Nester say, "Anger felt is no longer anger turned inward and directed against the self. And this will cause a decrease in the depression. It is not easy to be depressed and angry at the same time."[5]

As you learned in the last chapter, anger can energize you to make corrective changes in your life. Search your heart and see if you're allowing others to transgress your boundaries. Explore the possibility that the anger will provide the power you need to make critical changes in your life.

The Valley of the Shadow of Death

Certainly the psalmist had it right: Depression can make us feel as if we are walking through the valley of the shadow of death. If anyone could accurately depict the horrors of depression, David could. His words ring eerily true for the depressed person.

But David is not passively awaiting his demise as he writes Psalm 23. He acknowledges that even in the darkest times, of which he had many, he is confident that God will lead him and keep him safe. He has an abiding trust in God.

Try this exercise. Put each of the following phrases (from Psalm 23) into your own words. The Lord will…

- make me lie down in green pastures
- lead me beside still waters
- restore my soul
- guide me in paths of righteousness
- comfort me
- anoint my head with oil
- ensure that goodness and mercy follow me
- allow me to dwell in the house of the Lord forever

If this chapter finds you in difficult times, you can gain comfort in knowing that the same God who protected David will protect you. Notice that David felt protected even in the presence of his enemies. He wrote many of the psalms while in the midst of battle or while being pursued by Saul. He had reasons to be dismayed, and he succumbed to those feelings at times. But he kept coming back to his faith in Almighty God to be his shield.

The same God that watched over David is watching over you. He cares about your feelings and doesn't want you stuck in a state of depression. Take special note of your feelings and see what remedial action may spring from them.

9

Fear: From Enemy to Ally

All of us are born with a set of instinctive fears—
of falling, of the dark, of lobsters, of falling on lobsters
in the dark, or speaking before a Rotary Club,
and of the words "Some assembly required."

DAVE BARRY

We were ecstatic. My wife and I had just signed the papers on the purchase of an idyllic waterfront cottage on Bainbridge Island.

Having walked through countless unaffordable homes, witnessing how "the other half" lives, and ogling their incredible Seattle skyline views, we never thought we'd find something so nice within our budget. We warned the Realtors that they were probably wasting their time showing us homes because we simply couldn't swing what we wanted financially.

Undaunted, Mike and Robin were the consummate patient purveyors of property. They understood our love of Bainbridge Island (they lived on the island too) as well as the challenge of finding something in our price range.

We reached the point where we couldn't stand hearing the term *fixer-upper,* yet Mike and Robin continued to encourage us.

"We'll just keep our eyes and ears open," they said. "Something will turn up."

And it did.

One Sunday afternoon we received a call from Mike. "We found something you might want to see," he said with a hint of excitement.

"What've you got?" I asked.

"Just the most adorable cottage on the island," he said. "It's small, with only 25 feet of waterfront. But it would be *your* 25 feet, with nobody blocking your view. Do you want to take a look?"

"When can we see it?"

"Give me an hour, and I'll get a showing arranged this afternoon."

I called to Christie, who was downstairs working on a project, and shared the news.

"I see a field trip in our very near future," Christie said. We readied ourselves for an excursion, and when the phone call came indicating that the cottage was ready for us to see, we whisked out the door.

The home was a delightful 1930s bungalow with an angular view of the Seattle skyline. The owner was an interior designer whose impeccable color choices and accessories nearly caused Christie to stop breathing. Soft earth tones created a peaceful interior, and the huge rhododendrons, azaleas, and reflection pond made a stunning, bucolic landscape.

We couldn't hide our excitement. The layout was wonderful, the design exactly suited our taste, and the waterfront view was incredible. As we finished our tour, the pinkish hue of the Seattle skyline was beginning to come to life.

But there was one sizeable problem.

The cottage had our name all over it, but the price was out of our comfort zone. We spent the next two hours with Mike and Robin at a nearby restaurant talking about *creative financing*—a euphemism for finding a way to borrow more than you can afford.

Over the next few days we ran the numbers through our minds dozens of times, exploring ways to make it work. Real estate in this area would not decline in value, and to own any piece of property on Bainbridge Island seemed like an immense gift.

We prayed for wisdom. We pondered, considered, reflected, and prayed some more. Finally, at a meeting with a mortgage broker, we ran the numbers again and decided to make an offer. To our surprise, it was accepted. The cottage was ours!

We needed to sell some other property, and we would be a bit pinched until that transaction closed. But another Realtor told us that our property would sell quickly. We'd be out on a limb for a while, but we would be okay in the long run. We felt good about our decision.

And then it happened.

I bolted awake in the middle of the night with tightness in my chest, restless and unable to go back to sleep. What had we done? Would we really be able to make the mortgage payments? What if the other property didn't sell? Could we end up losing our primary residence? Suddenly, I was consumed by the thought that we had been suckered into buying something beyond our means.

I turned to Christie and noticed that she was awake as well.

"What are you doing up?" I asked.

"I can't sleep," she said. "I'm excited about the cottage, but I wonder if we've bitten off more than we can chew. I really want that cottage, but maybe this isn't the right time for us."

Together we lay awake, our bodies sending chemical messengers into our systems—primarily dopamine and adrenaline. The reaction was similar to the one we'd have had if we were being burglarized or facing imminent danger. Cortisol was pulsing through our bodies, with blood sugar and blood pressure rising sharply, giving us an unwanted burst of energy. Not exactly what we desired at 2:00 a.m., but it was exactly what we needed.

We lay together for an hour or so, sharing our concerns. Our fear was real. It was also helpful. We reconsidered our decision and decided to place another lot we owned up for sale, giving us the breathing room we needed to make the Dalnbridge purchase. We also decided to rent out the cottage at times, which would help us make the mortgage payment. These changes in our game plan helped us calm down and move ahead more confidently with our purchase.

Christie and I had listened to our fear and learned from it—all a part of emotional decision making. As a result, we allowed our anxiety to steer us toward corrective choices.

False Evidence Appearing Real

Fear isn't always as helpful as it was to Christie and me that night several months ago. Sometimes fear can be an enemy, not an ally.

I was on a routine flight from Seattle to Chicago, and being an experienced traveler, I thought nothing of the initial turbulence. Flight attendants often encourage pasengers to fasten their seat belts when things get a little bumpy.

But this felt different. The plane started bouncing around like an old bus on a rutted Mexican road. I was trying to use my laptop but soon found this impossible. Before I could turn it off, it slid off the tray and into my lap.

Then I heard the whir of the engines slow.

My heart rate shot up, and my breathing become shallow. My edginess was on a direct course toward fear as my body prepared to face imminent danger. I continued to tell myself this was just a bumpy ride and that I had nothing to worry about.

The plane lurched and heaved, creating more bouncing than I had ever experienced on a flight. This was not routine turbulence for me, and I'm a seasoned flyer. Just as I was trying to settle my nerves, the captain came on the speaker.

"Hello, folks," he said calmly. "As you can tell, we've hit some choppy air and are getting bounced around pretty nicely. They're telling us there's smoother air down around twenty-eight thousand feet, and we're going to check that out. There's nothing to be concerned about, and we'll get through this in just a few minutes. In the meantime, keep those seat belts securely fastened. We'll keep you posted from the flight deck."

Whew! Nothing like the calm voice from the person with the yoke in his hands! Instantly, I felt better.

I glanced at the man seated next to me, who was fumbling with his seat belt.

"So this is choppy air?" I joked. "I'd hate to see what significant turbulence is like."

"I guess he knows more about this stuff than we do," the man said. "Maybe that's why he's the pilot. To the guy who knows exactly what that air means and how to handle it, I suppose it's just an annoyance. To guys like us, it can be a little disconcerting."

Though no one knew what I was experiencing, I felt embarrassed. Intellectually, I knew this was only turbulence and that today's jetliners are built to slice through the "choppy air" with ease. But at moments like these, we can very easily fall victim to FEAR—False Evidence Appearing Real.

This is the problem with fear. Our perceptions and judgments are based on far more than reality, and the same set of circumstances can trigger different responses. Thus, we have to refine our emotional decision-making skills if they are to work effectively. Our challenge is to listen to our emotions and yet carefully check the perceptions that lead to our conclusions. Failing to do that, we run the danger of emotional reaction or, at the other extreme, compartmentalizing our feelings.

The Many Faces of Fear

Fear may be the most powerful force for altering human behavior. It sharpens our vision and heightens our readiness for action, but it can also paralyze us. Our immediate fight-or-flight response, bred into us over time, can be very useful. When our fear response continues too long, however, we can become exhausted. Our goal is to perfect our ability to know when to fight, when to flee, and when to simply relax. Fear can be a beneficial emotion when we use it properly. But it can be an incredibly damaging emotion when we let it run amok.

One of our main problems with fear is that it often lurks in the recesses of our minds. When it is out in the open, as when I awakened in the middle of a dead sleep because of my worries about the purchase of the Bainbridge cottage, it alerts us to changes we need to make. In my case, fear was an ally. It forced Christie and me to revamp our game plan so we were living within our comfort zone.

Many people have similar experiences in which fear helps them meet real danger. Fear speeds up blood flow to every part of our bodies, allowing us to act quickly to meet danger head-on. Fear warns us that serious trouble may be ahead. Fear alerts us to relational problems that we need to address and addictions that are eating away at our lives. It also signals that our bodies need a tune-up. Fear can literally be a lifesaver, as Gavin De Becker, an authority on this subject, writes in his bestselling book *The Gift of Fear:*

> Real fear is a signal intended to be very brief, a mere servant of intuition. But though few would argue that extended, unanswered fear is destructive, millions choose to stay there…True fear is a survival signal that sounds only in the presence of danger, yet unwarranted fear has assumed a power over us that it holds over no other creature on earth…It need not be this way.[1]

Fear can clearly be a destroyer and robber, as with the moments stolen from me in the airplane. Though I was not in danger, I slipped quickly into survival mode. We were simply in "choppy air" and required only the sure hands of a pilot who had handled similar circumstances hundreds of times before.

Fear can present itself as either an enemy or an ally, and we must learn to discern the difference. Our challenge is to decide if the pounding in our chest and the restricting of our pupils indicate a time for fight or flight, or if it is simply False Evidence Appearing Real. Learning to determine the difference is a critical skill.

Let's examine some of the faces of fear we're likely to encounter. Then we'll explore those we're not likely to find unless we go on a hunting expedition.

Unhealthy Fear

I've never met anyone who didn't have some unhealthy fears. As De Becker says, we've let fear run our lives. We may think our anxieties are unique, but that's rarely the case. Undoubtedly, you have your own list of people, places, and situations that strike fear in your heart. Your fears are very real to you. To some extent, they paralyze you and prevent you from making healthy emotional decisions.

Here are a few typical unhealthy, paralyzing fears:

- *Animals and insects.* Many people have an irrational fear of animals or insects that are relatively harmless. My wife is terrified of mice (dead or alive). I am afraid of snakes (alive).

- *Heights.* Many people have some uneasiness or even an overwhelming fear of heights.

- *Rejection.* No one likes being rejected, but some people become obsessed with protecting themselves from rejection.

- *Public speaking.* This ranks as the number one fear among us. Some people would rather dive into a pit of snakes than get up in front of a crowd and speak.

- *Flying.* Some people are so afraid of flying that they'll take a slow boat or train to reach a far-off destination.

- *Being alone.* People who can't stand being by themselves often act on the urge to merge, regardless of the cost.

- *Intimacy.* Countless people have been hurt one too many times and have decided never to be hurt again.

- *Closed spaces.* Most people have some discomfort about being in closed spaces, but some actually panic or become claustrophobic when trapped in a small, enclosed area.

Of course the list could go on and on. Unhealthy fear is a misguided, overreactive emotion. On the other hand, healthy fear protects us, motivates us, and changes circumstances for the better.

Healthy Fear

Unhealthy fear is a knee-jerk response to danger that doesn't really exist. Conversely, healthy fear is the same automatic response to *real* danger. My reaction in the middle of the night was an example of healthy, helpful fear. My reaction to the bouncy flight was unhealthy, unnecessary emotion. Let's consider some of the positive fears we face in our lives.

- *Violence.* We should be cautious about potentially violent people. When passing through areas of high crime, we are right to be cautious and perhaps even a bit fearful.

- *Physical pain.* We are wise to have a healthy respect for activities and circumstances that can cause us physical pain.

- *Speed.* We should understand that speed kills, and we must be cautious about traveling at unsafe or uncomfortable speeds.

- *Emotional ridicule and shame.* Certain people cannot be trusted with our emotions. We are wise to be wary of them.

- *Imminent danger.* We should respond immediately when we're in true danger. Being safe includes having a healthy fear of electricity, hurricanes, tidal waves, and the like.

Healthy fear is like a caution light on our emotional dashboards. When we face a situation that contains imminent danger, our warning light of fear comes on, offering us invaluable information. Sometimes these warning lights literally save our lives. We learn about situations that are dangerous to us, people who can harm us emotionally or physically, and other circumstances of concern. Fear becomes a primary tool for effective emotional decision making.

The Hidden Faces of Fear

Knowing your fears and either facing or avoiding the situations that prompt them—that's good. Having those fears mucking around in your unconscious and driving your everyday behavior—that's bad. These nebulous apprehensions are not healthy or helpful in our emotional decision making.

I've said repeatedly that the feelings we deny will be intensified in our lives. In other words, if we don't give voice to our feelings, they will control us. One way or another, they're going to have their day.

My goal in this book is to strongly encourage you to embrace your emotions and utilize that energy in motion for healthy decision making. Fear provides one of the most potent bundles of energy available to us for positive change. But before we can tap into it, we must become aware of how this same fear saps our strength and energy if we deny and avoid it.

Think about it. When these unspoken, unrecognized fears lurk just below the surface, we're using our energy to subvert them. As the pressure mounts, we use more and more effort to keep the lid on. We eventually feel depleted and exhausted.

Consider some of these other signs of hidden fears:

- *Low self-esteem.* In many cases, fear is at the heart of low self-esteem. People who struggle with self-esteem issues often fear being known by others. They are caught in a vicious cycle of disliking themselves, hiding that self from others and then disliking themselves all the more. This often takes place subconsciously.

- *Habitual avoidance.* Many find themselves caught in a web of avoidance, never really taking the time to examine and explore their fears. They've been avoiding people, places, and circumstances for so long that doing so has become second nature. The avoidance that accompanies this paralysis only reinforces the power of the fear.

- *Negativity.* Show me someone who is a chronic complainer, downcast and negative about life, and I'll show you someone with a boatload of hidden fears. Were you to ask him if he's afraid, he would probably deny it. Don't believe him. Beneath that tough facade is a frightened child who sees only the dark side of life.

- *Arrogance.* Just as negativity is a sure sign of hidden fearfulness, arrogance often is a sign of the opposite—insecurity. When people don't feel safe sharing their insecurity and apprehension, they are likely to promote themselves a lot. To be human is to be fearful at times.

- *Hypochondriasis.* You know the type. They have every illness known to humankind, and if they haven't gotten it, they will. Many times, these individuals cannot name their true fears, and thus problems become "somatized"—expressed in their bodies. Psychosomatic illness is rampant as we struggle with naming, embracing, and learning from our fears.

- *Perfectionism.* Many perfectionists work overtime to be the best, brightest, richest, and most accomplished folks on the block. Why? Because underlying fears they cannot name or embrace take their unconscious toll. Afraid to face their fears, perfectionists drive themselves mercilessly, hoping to achieve unrealistic goals.

- *Confusion.* Confused people are often afraid of seeing things as they are. They are unwilling to acknowledge their fears and take appropriate action. They envision too many details and too many possibilities, and they are too frightened to make decisions.

- *Spiritualizers.* Super-spirituality, or religious zealotry, is often a cloak of denial, covering spiritual and emotional insecurity. Having a pat answer for everything, these extremists are often intolerant of differences or of those who disagree with them. Spiritually mature individuals leave room for mystery and doubt, and they don't need to pretend that everything is fine, under control, understandable, and acceptable at all times.

The *only* way to heal fear is to feel it. Denial of any of our emotions leads to trouble. Although I don't want to wish fear on anyone, it's part of life.

As Susan Jeffers says in her bestselling book *Feel the Fear...and Do It Anyway,* we stop experiencing fear when we stop breathing. To stop feeling fear means we're either dead, well-anesthetized, in denial, or living with a tremendous layer of insulation.[2]

Seeking Safety

Fear is such an uncomfortable feeling that many of us develop creative ways to avoid it. Rather than face our fears and learn from them, we would rather hide. We insulate ourselves, seeking safety, instead of pressing ourselves to grow beyond our fears. Real or false, fear sends most of us into hiding.

Rhonda Britton, in her book *Fearless Living*, explains how we set ourselves up to be even more fearful by always seeking safety in our lives. One of the ways we do this, she says, is by being...

> a prisoner of the wishing, waiting, hoping trio of expectations. Wishing, the first stage of this mechanism for avoiding reality, involves immature and magical thinking reminiscent of a child blowing out candles on a birthday cake and really believing the silent request will come true. Waiting, the second stage, is when you sit back and assume that your desires will be fulfilled even if you do absolutely nothing to make that happen. Hoping, the final stage, is a desperate, aching kind of inner pleading that kicks in when you have to admit to yourself time is slipping by and your wish isn't getting any results.[3]

Notice the passivity involved in this kind of magical thinking. Apprehensive people often wish and hope their fears will dissipate without having to change their lives.

Fearful people are often passive in other areas as well. Listen to their typical language:

- They say they can't rather than they won't.

- They blame others for their problems, playing the victim rather than taking responsibility for their lives.

- They avoid frightening situations rather than courageously leaning into the circumstances that bring them fear.

- They feel powerless to change their lives rather than addressing the challenges they must overcome.

Our fears don't simply disappear. We must take real action, face our fears, and make changes in our lives. We must refuse to be paralyzed by our anxieties.

Baby Steps: Growth Through Fear

I'm aware of the counsel that tells us that climbing back on the buckin' bronco is the best way to move from fear to courageous living. That may work for some, but I'm more comfortable with baby steps. When I've been bucked off some "bronco" in my life, fear immediately takes up residence within. I need time to lick my wounds, survey the territory, and determine my next course of action.

This seems to be the case for many of my clients as well. Jackie was one such example.

Jackie is a 45-year-old double-divorcée whose second marriage ended four years ago. With lively, spiked brown hair and bright, blue eyes, she generally leans into life. She's been dating for the past two years but has been unsuccessful in finding "qualified men."

"I'm tired of trying to locate the right guy," she said with obvious irritation. "I've already picked two losers, and I don't want to do that again. I'm making a good salary, I've traveled, and I own my own home. It's all coming together for me, but I'm afraid of choosing another dope. So I've given up on dating. But the problem is that I don't like the loneliness."

Jackie is an attractive, bright woman. A quick review of her history clearly revealed, however, that she had relational problems. Skilled at her job as a project manager for a chemical company, she proudly told me she had started with a high school education and learned to work "in a man's world, just like a man." The irony was that while she was able to stand up to men, she was unable to create a loving relationship with one.

"What would you like to work on?" I asked.

"The obvious," she said. "I know I've learned to protect myself from being hurt. I find ways to sabotage relationships, and I know it's time to ask for help."

"Let's talk about how you sabotage relationships," I said.

"My first two marriages were a joke. Both my husbands were alcoholics, and both cheated on me. I should have seen it coming, but I didn't. Denial, I guess. Still, I stuck around for years. When I figured things out and got rid of the first one, I found another one just like him."

"We tend to repeat patterns when we don't realize what we're doing," I said.

"That's the strange thing," she said. "I think I was aware of what I was doing. I knew I could control both of my husbands, even though they thought they were controlling me. I knew how to manipulate them. I never had to be really vulnerable with either of them. In a strange way, I was safe with them."

"So you're frightened about really getting close to men?"

"Bingo," she said. "I like to pretend I'm tough and can talk their language."

"Explain that to me."

"Men. Hard men. Tough men. I know how to relate to them," she said. "I learned how from my dad, and believe me, he's a case too."

"But now you think you're ready to face your fears? You're ready to learn to actually be vulnerable in a relationship?"

"I'd love to say yes, and that I'm ready to choose a very different man. But it's going to be scary. I'd love to attract a different kind of guy. Someone who will really love me. Someone who will come home to me at night. Someone I can love with my whole heart. That's what I want."

"It can happen," I said. "It will take some work, but we're never too old to change our patterns. It will take moving ahead slowly, changing old patterns and being aware of the fears that arise in the process."

Jackie has attended counseling for three months now and hasn't missed a session. We talked about her father and the abuse she experienced from him. We talked about the pain she still carried from her two marriages and the frustration of dating these past two years. We talked a lot about her fears—the fear that she wouldn't be able to attract a nice man, the fear of being unable to allow a man to get close to her, the fear of being unable to forgive someone who might hurt her. Jackie found that talking about her apprehension was very helpful. The more she discussed her fears, the less powerful they became.

Jackie also made some decisions in counseling. She decided to stand up to her fear instead of allowing it to paralyze her. She decided to manage her anxiety, take calculated and appropriate risks, and press forward. She joined a Christian dating program in her town and dated men who shared her faith. Today, she feels more hopeful than ever because she listened to her fear and took decisive action to manage it.

Winds and Waves

I am encouraged when I read accounts of the disciples because they sound a lot like me. They had been with Jesus for some time, they had seen His miracles, and they knew He was fully capable of managing the most difficult circumstances, but this had little influence on them when facing a storm on the Sea of Galilee.

> Leaving the crowd behind, they took him along, just as he was, in the boat. There were also other boats with him. A furious squall came up, and the waves broke over the boat, so that it was nearly swamped. Jesus was in the stern, sleeping on a cushion. The disciples woke him and said to him, "Teacher, don't you care if we drown?"
>
> He got up, rebuked the wind and said to the waves, "Quiet! Be still." Then the wind died down and it was completely calm.
>
> He said to his disciples, "Why are you so afraid? Do you still have no faith?"
>
> They were terrified and asked each other, "Who is this? Even the wind and the waves obey him!" (Mark 4:36-41).

When the disciples faced a storm, they felt afraid and panicked.

The surprising thing about this story is that the disciples had spent their lives on this body of water and were quite familiar with the unexpected tempests that could arise. Yet they panicked. They had spent a great deal of time with Jesus and had seen many of His miracles. Yet they underestimated Him.

In one respect, their fear was understandable. This was a violent storm, fully capable of causing them harm. However, their fear was also False Evidence Appearing Real because the Master of the wind and waves was with them. Their fear revealed their lack of trust. Jesus is capable of handling these crises, but we must place our trust in Him.

How was their fear instructional? How could it become a valuable part of their emotional decision making?

The disciples' apprehension caused them to wake Jesus. They sensed danger, and their fear pushed them to take appropriate action. However, that same fear also revealed to Jesus that their faith needed to grow. The storm was a test, and they failed it because their panic was evidence of a lack of conviction. Jesus challenged them to grow in their faith.

Our fears offer the same opportunity to explore what we place our trust in and how much we really trust Jesus to guide us through the storms of life. Are we subjected to dangerous situations? Of course. But after we have experienced enough of these squalls and witnessed Jesus' ability to rule over them, we learn to trust Him to safely take us through them.

What are your fears? Are they healthy fears that alert you to dangerous situations, or are they unhealthy, paralyzing fears? Listen carefully to them. They can assist you in healthy emotional decision making and help you to grow!

10

Sadness: Pathway to Healing

*When you are sorrowful look again in your heart,
and you shall see that in truth you are weeping for
that which has been your delight.*

KAHLIL GIBRAN

Life is filled with losses, large and small, that often lead to feelings of sadness. At any given time, something in our lives is giving birth and something is dying. Sometimes we feel these losses and move on. But often they settle into our subconscious unnoticed.

Such is certainly the case in my life.

As I write this chapter, I'm aware of many undercurrents of loss. I feel sad that my two sons live across the country and miss them very much as they build their adult lives. At the same time, I live much closer to my aging parents and helplessly watch as their health declines.

I don't like these changes even though they are normal undulations and losses of life. I sometimes wish for days from the past when my sons were young and bounced around the house with unbridled energy. They brought vigor to my life, inviting friends and mischief into our home in large doses.

I reminisce about their first day of school, their first T-ball game, their first academic and athletic honors, their first girlfriends, their first days away from home, and their first trip to college. Many parents are exuberant when their kids leave the nest—I wasn't. Although I am proud of their many accomplishments, my role in their lives has diminished.

Likewise, I reminisce about old times in my family of origin, days when my parents were young and vibrant. I recall boating in the San Juan Islands and frolicking on Silver Lake, where our family owned a cabin. I remember my antics with buddies on Nevada Street, the only home I knew growing up in Bellingham, Washington.

I'm also saddened by my younger sister's struggle with cancer. I call to let her know I'm thinking of her and praying for her, but it doesn't seem enough. I want the cancer to go away; I want her to be in good health.

On a broader scale, I'm troubled about the losses we experience as a nation: the tragic shooting at Virginia Tech and the war in Iraq, which has taken a huge toll. For the most part, however, the majority of us will not be immediately touched by these losses. We will shake our heads, reflect, and move on with our lives. Busyness and denial create an emotional barrier between us and these crises. We cannot, however, help but feel the losses that impact us personally on a daily basis. Ironically, this sadness brings another opportunity for healthy emotional decision making.

Sadness and the losses that bring it about are opportunities for us to tune in to our feelings and make decisions from them. Sadness, like our other emotions, gives a rich texture to life. Although I miss my sons and certainly don't enjoy watching my parents' health decline, these circumstances offer the potential for reflection. These losses make me aware of what is important in my life.

What Is Sadness?

Sadness is an unpleasant, visceral feeling of sorrow, unhappiness, or gloom characterized by drooping eyelids, flaccid muscles, hanging head, contracted chest, and lowered lips, cheeks, and jaw. Individuals who are sad are often passive and appear lifeless.

Sadness results when people have lost something important or when they're disappointed about something. We feel sad when we lose a friend, experience a death, or simply feel misunderstood. We also share sadness with friends and family members when they've experienced a significant loss in their lives.

To feel that sadness is overwhelming us is not unusual. During such moments, the world may seem like an unfriendly place. Sadness may drift into discouragement, obliterating any positive feelings we had been experiencing.

When sad, we may feel like crying or even weeping uncontrollably. The turmoil usually starts with a distressing thought, memory, or experience, and it can lead to tears and restricted breathing. Actually, crying can be good for us. Once we've had a good cry, we may begin to come to terms with the experience. Many people experience relief after they've cried.

Let's consider a few situations that typically lead to sadness.

Loss and separation. We naturally feel sadness when facing loss or separation from someone or something important to us. Almost all sorrow can be traced to loss of one kind or another. It may be the loss of an important friendship, a death in our family, the loss of a pet, or perhaps even something as simple as losing an object that was important to us.

Changes. Changes often bring about feelings of sadness. Even changes for the good can prompt this reaction. People who experience demotions or promotions commonly feel a sense of sadness at the change because every change brings about loss in one form or another. Physical moves from one home to another, one city to another, or even one church to another prompt feelings of sadness. Again, these feelings, marked by adjustments in our lives, often signify some sort of loss.

As I mentioned earlier, my wife and I made a major purchase

of a home on Bainbridge Island, so we had to sell some view property on Hood Canal where we had spent many magical evenings. I pondered this move for hours, tuning in to my ambivalence and anticipatory grief over the sale. Although we were delighted with our new purchase, it meant saying goodbye to a place where we had enjoyed some wonderful memories. I felt sad for some time about selling that property.

Disappointments. We sometimes wish for certain outcomes to events. We hope for a result, and if it doesn't come to pass, we feel sadness and despair.

I worked with a man recently who had expected to receive a promotion at work. He was so sure of his advancement that he began dreaming of what he would do with the extra money he'd earn from the new job.

When he learned that he had been passed over for the promotion, he was severely depressed. He even considered resigning from his position in the company. Although he initially felt overwhelmed with sadness, he confronted the pain, and within a fairly short period of time, he was back to his old self.

Relationship struggles. Perhaps nothing causes so much sadness as relationship struggles. Relationships are where we spend the majority of our life's energies. When they are going well, we're happy; when not, we are miserable. Because relationships are so central to our lives, we are particularly vulnerable to experiencing sadness when they are not functioning properly.

This list of causes for sadness is certainly not exhaustive. There are as many reasons for unhappiness as there are personalities—and there are many. In each of these examples, however, we see that emotions—energy in motion—can help us make important decisions in our lives. Whether we are feeling down about a loss in our lives or feeling sad about some aspect of our marriage that is distressing, understanding and embracing our sadness can help us discern what changes we need to make to return to optimal functioning.

Common Inhibiting Beliefs

Those who resist unpleasant emotions may fear sadness for a number of irrational reasons. They may entertain unhelpful thoughts like these:

If I feel sad, I'll start crying and never stop. The truth of the matter, of course, is that we very well may start crying, but we will certainly stop. This untrue thought probably reveals that we actually fear a loss of control. We are unable to simply turn off our feelings, so they temporarily overtake us. But we will stop crying when we have finished grieving.

Crying is a sign of weakness. This belief seems to have its roots in cultures that prize self-control. Men in particular have been taught that they should never be seen crying, so they repress their sadness and tears, causing further problems. When we stifle one emotion, we inhibit others as well.

The truth of the matter is that feeling sadness and shedding tears are not signs of weakness. They are actually signs of emotional health. Expressing our emotions requires courage and strength. It helps us to be authentic, and this certainly aids in the cultivation of healthy relationships.

No one wants to see me cry. This is actually partly true. Men are especially uncomfortable with sorrow, so they don't like seeing their mate experience this tender emotion. But that should not keep us from feeling and expressing our sadness.

We commonly hear people refer to crying as "breaking down in tears" as if crying were some form of emotional collapse. Crying is not a breakdown; it's the body's natural response to loss. To feel this emotion and integrate the sadness and losses into your consciousness so that you can make sense of what is happening is a healthy process.

Grief Is the Healing Feeling

When I feel sadness and succumb to feelings of grief, I am reassured to know that healing will be part of the process. I learned in both graduate school and the school of hard knocks that grief is the healing feeling. Sorrow and grief are integrally connected.

Whenever we allow ourselves to attend to our sadness and follow its natural course of grieving, we will ultimately feel better. Anguish is like a container of pain carried deep within that must be emptied periodically. If we don't unload it by grieving, we carry around the weight of our unresolved losses, both large and small.

Howard Clinebell, in his book *Well Being,* reveals five tasks—or emotional decision-making opportunities—for healing from grief.[1] He uses the term *grief work,* which was coined by Erich Lindemann. Dealing effectively with grief can be real work, and yet when done correctly, it helps us move along with our lives. Consider how these five tasks might apply to losses in your life.

Accept Reality

First, gradually let go of denial and accept the painful reality of the problem or loss. Clinebell notes, "When something traumatic hits us like a ton of bricks, our minds mercifully protect us from overload by the psychological defense of denial." But for healing to take place, the layer of denial must give way to reality. We must feel the immensity of our loss—perhaps a step at a time.

Many people get confused about the issue of feeling the fullness of their sadness, believing that it is a "once and for all" phenomenon. Unfortunately, this is not the case. Sadness often comes in waves that gradually decrease. Sometimes the smaller, later waves surprise us because we believed we were finished with our grief. But it may take a long time to spend itself, and we must be patient.

Any loss, large or small, causes sadness at some level. Small, daily losses can accumulate, leading to feelings of sorrow. An interpersonal rejection here, a missed opportunity there, and an embarrassing mistake can all take their toll. We must not deny the power of small losses in our lives.

Express Your Feelings

Second, experience and express fully your agonizing feelings, talking about them until you gradually release them. It has been said that we need to talk about our losses 100 times. Many patients scoff when I share this advice with them, but I have found, both personally and professionally, that we do need to talk and talk and talk about our grief. Far too many people are unwilling to do this. But when feelings have to live underground, they eventually pop out in various disguises.

Preposterous, you say? You've grieved enough. The loss was long ago, and so much time has gone by. You know you shouldn't be sad after all this time, but you can't seem to let the feelings go.

Talk about it.

But what if you've already cried about that loss that sent you reeling years ago? The unexpected divorce is history, and you want to put it away and move on with life. That firing that took you completely off guard, crushing your feelings and pride, was months in the past. Why are you still feeling punky, you wonder?

Talk about it. Talk about it. Talk about it.

Through talking we not only gain a greater understanding of our pain and loss, integrating them into our life, but also receive critical support and safety for processing our issues.

Even if you buy what I'm saying and decide that you need to discuss those losses that continue to rob your sleep and invade your conscious life, to whom do you turn? You've already talked to your friends and family, and you're convinced they are tired of listening to you.

This is usually not true. Rarely have we burdened our friends and family as much as we imagine. We're the ones who are tired of our sadness, not them. We're the ones worrying about how much time we've asked them to spend sitting with us while we tell our story one more time.

Your friends are often willing to listen, and they may even count it a privilege to share in your loss. Alexandra Stoddard writes about this in her book *Living a Beautiful Life:* "Sharing doubles joy and diminishes sorrow…. sharing requires participation; when we share, we give a portion of our gifts to someone else…In the happiness of loving another, we feel better about ourselves as well."[2]

What do we need from our friends and family? We need someone to listen without judging. Not everyone can do this, and you know which friends and family can actually be there for you when you are vulnerable with them. To truly share our sorrow, we need someone who will encourage us to talk about it again and again.

When doing grief work, we run a risk of trying to keep our feelings sanitized. After all, as we're expressing our sorrow, anger and even rage may come pouring forth. The able listener is willing to allow and even encourage us to express these messy and conflicted feelings. Even though we probably played a part in that broken friendship, we need to express our unmitigated grief in raw form. Political incorrectness may bubble out. This is not necessarily a time for us to worry about speaking with sensitivity, and the listening friend or family member must be willing to accept that this is a time to simply say it. Examination will come later.

Seek the listener who will, as Clinebell says, "create an inviting silence into which the person can pour the bitter brew of rage, longing, remorse, confusion, self-pity, hopelessness, denial, emptiness, disorientation, and in some cases, relief, release, and hope. Listening in this depth is the gift."[3]

Rebuilding

Third, put your life back together gradually, in some workable form, without whatever you have lost. This is a significant challenge. After we lose an important job, suffer through a broken marriage, or face the future following the death of a loved one, rebuilding our life is the last thing we want to do. But we must do it if we are to move ourselves beyond paralysis.

I spoke recently with a client named Sandy who had received a "Dear Jane" letter. Nearly a year had passed since her boyfriend, Kyle, broke her heart, yet she could not seem to move forward with her life. She wondered how she could ever get past her grief, given the immensity of her loss.

Sandy shared how she had fallen madly in love with Kyle. They had a whirlwind romance and were talking about marriage within months of their initial meeting. Everything clicked; he was a gentle, loving man, and he was financially stable and owned his own business. He lived in a neighboring city, and they saw each other on weekends. They were both strong Christians and vowed to save themselves sexually for marriage. Their resolve lasted several months, she said, and then in a moment of passion they slipped. This was not the end of the relationship, however, and seemed to add even more urgency and importance to getting married.

As talk of marriage heated, Kyle grew more distant. His calls became less frequent, and he found reasons to cancel several dates. Sandy felt the relationship dissolving but feared confronting him about what she was sensing. Eventually, she broached the topic with Kyle, but he yielded few answers and grew even more distant. Finally, she stopped hearing from him.

Her heart was broken, and she is still struggling to get on with life.

"How can I go forward when I still love Kyle?" she asked. "He was the man of my dreams and everything I wanted in a husband. We planned our future together. I can't imagine dating again when so much of me still belongs to him."

Sandy is stuck in her grief. This is understandable, given the immensity of her loss. In some sense, this kind of overwhelming circumstance affects us forever. We have given part of our hearts to another, so we will always carry a wound. Yet Sandy must begin to piece her life back together. She must begin the process of creating a life without Kyle. She must retrace her steps and consider reengaging herself in the activities she was involved with before they met. She must connect with her friends, participate in hobbies that she enjoys, and simply put one foot in front of the other while she heals.

Sandy must simultaneously embrace and explore her sadness. Buried in her pain may be clues to why she feels stuck. Is she afraid she can never love again? Does she feel unlovable after this rejection? Perhaps she has compounded her sadness by refusing to embrace her anger. She will discover the next step in decision making as she explores and understands her feelings.

Find Meaning

Fourth, stretch your faith to find some meaning in your new situation. Losses create a powerful environment for spiritual growth. Although none of us wish to incur losses, they prompt us to turn to God for help.

> Crises expose the inadequacies of our little gods, the values we have worshiped by our lifestyles like achievements, success, security, power, prestige and possessions. Crises invite us to see our idols as unworthy of being given so much of our precious passion and devotion.[4]

Any loss brings a temptation to blame God for not protecting us. Whether we admit it or not, many of us believe that if we are good or loving enough, we won't face adversity. When adversity strikes, we feel betrayed. But God never promised that we are immune from loss. Quite the opposite.

> It is better to go to a house of mourning than to go to a house of feasting, for death is the destiny of every man...Sorrow is better than laughter, because a sad face is good for the heart (Ecclesiastes 7:2-3).

What kind of counsel is this, you might wonder? Perhaps you thought the Christian life was always joyful. Not true. Although we are to enjoy what we have while we have it, we must be aware that these blessings are on loan to us. We must remember, Solomon warns, that suffering and sorrow will strike every person, and these times can serve as refining fire for our character. We will learn lessons through adversity that we could never learn in times of blessing.

Reach Out

Fifth, join hands with others who are going through similar problems, giving each other mutual understanding and help. We desperately need each other, especially during times of sorrow. We simply cannot navigate these times alone, nor should we try. We receive experience, strength, and hope when we share with others who have experienced or are experiencing similar circumstances.

As Robert Fulgham so aptly said, "When you go out in the world, watch out for traffic, hold hands, and stick together."[5] Fulgham spoke in language we could all understand, and his advice is right on the money. Most of us have heard similar instructions from our elementary teachers, parents, or Sunday school teachers. Stick together. Hold hands. Life is better when we are connected to one another.

We sometimes need to sit with those who have experienced similar crises in their lives. When people suffer a divorce, attending a divorce recovery group where others have experienced similar marital problems can be extremely helpful. Although they may have friends supporting them who have never been divorced, people in trauma can experience something powerful when they are with those who share their pain. They can rant and rave, weep and cry out. The people in the group have been there and know how each other feels. This is a healing experience.

Healthy Sadness and Grief

Sadness is typically a natural aspect of grieving. However, most people don't know what to expect when entering into grief. A normal grief process has definable steps, and simply knowing this may help you as you navigate losses in your life.

- *Shock and numbness.* During this phase we simply don't want to acknowledge the loss. Our emotions and thoughts are overwhelmed, and we try to block out the reality of the situation.

- *Yearning and searching.* Still struggling to accept the reality of the loss, we wonder if it's all a dream. Maybe our loved one will return to us; maybe the bad news is simply a mistake.

- *Disorganization and despair.* As our world collapses, we cannot function normally. Our lives are disrupted, or worse, they are shattered, and we find it difficult to eat, sleep, or function at work.

- *Reorganization.* After some time we begin to put our lives back together. We allow ourselves to grieve the loss and then begin the process of piecing our new lives together.

Although we see an order to these steps, we commonly move back and forth through the process. For example, at one moment we may feel as if we've accepted the loss, grieved it, and moved on, when suddenly we feel ourselves slipping backward. Remember, these "sneaker waves" happen with every loss and are to be expected and even anticipated. Grief doesn't follow a predictable timetable. We grieve and heal at our own pace.

Buried Sadness

"I should be over it by now!" an elderly client exclaimed to me recently as she dabbed angrily at her tears. "It's been a year since my husband died. There's no bringing him back. "

"But you were married to him for 50 years," I said, "and you shared many wonderful memories with him."

"Some good and some not so good."

Thin and elegant, Jessica had lost 20 pounds in recent months, causing her physician concern and leading to her referral to me. She had neatly coiffed white hair and a spry, vivid spirit that I liked. But she was clearly "old school" about her feelings, believing they were private and meant to be dispensed with as quickly as possible.

"There's no sense crying at this point," she said sharply. "What's done is done, and now I've got to get on with things. Do you know how to bring back my husband, or even my appetite, for that matter?"

"Actually," I said, "I've got some ideas about that."

"Well, you'll be doing better than Dr. Jackson if you can get some weight back on me. He couldn't do a thing for me. I don't think anybody can, for that matter."

"The thing we *can* do, Jessica, is talk about the loss of your husband. And Dr. Jackson informed me that you've had some other losses recently as well, including your sister and a favorite pet."

"I knew my sister was going to die," Jessica stated matter-of-factly. "She's had cancer twice before. It was just a matter of time. My cat…"

Jessica paused, started to speak, and then buried her face in her handkerchief.

"I loved that cat," she said, "and I don't suppose you understand that. I raised her from a tiny kitten, and she's been my joy for the past 15 years. I miss her terribly."

For the next hour, Jessica and I talked about her husband, her sister, and her beloved cat. We talked about losses, about sadness, and most importantly, about how she didn't want to feel her grief.

Jessica left that day saying she felt better and reluctantly agreed to come back to talk with me. She admitted that burying her sadness might be playing a role in her weight loss, and that some good might come from talking about her feelings.

In order for Jessica to heal from her setbacks, she had to follow some important guidelines for dealing with sadness and loss. We must do the same.

- Embrace sadness. We cannot heal what we cannot feel.

- Try to be comfortable with the sadness. Erase thoughts about certain feelings being good and others being bad.

- Give up timelines for grieving. We're finished grieving when we're finished grieving and no sooner.

- Remember that the extent of our sadness and grief is commensurate with the importance of that loss in our lives.

- Be willing to cry as often and hard and long as necessary.

- Find support for the grief process. Seek healing communities where others have experienced similar losses.

Jessica's losses were compounded by their sheer number. She was dealing with not only the loss of her husband but also the loss of her sister and pet. As we explored her history, we discovered that she had other setbacks that she had not fully grieved. She had lost her parents several years earlier, and these losses were contributing to how she faced her current losses. When we refuse to grieve our losses, they add more fuel to each successive fire. Such was the case with Jessica.

A Complicated Grief Reaction

So you've embraced your sadness, softened some of the negative self-talk about not feeling these painful emotions, and even allowed yourself to cry. But still the sadness lingers. What can you do now? What happens when the grief and loss simply won't go away?

When our sadness becomes protracted, something may be amiss. Because of the immensity of the situation, you may find yourself overwhelmed and unable to cope. During these times, using your emotions for decision making becomes more challenging. When we simply cannot mobilize our normal resources to cope, something is wrong. When time, faith, and embracing our emotions bring no relief, we need to consider that we're experiencing what is called a *complicated grief reaction.*

A complicated grief reaction occurs when the emotional wound is infected. Just as a spiked fever warns us of an infection in our body, an ongoing spike in our emotions warrants attention as well. This eruption of emotions suggests unfinished business for a number of possible reasons.

- We may have idealized the lost object or person and refused to let go.
- We may feel overwhelmed by the immensity of the loss.
- We may have had multiple losses, each compounding and complicating the other.
- Our thoughts may have become muddled, keeping us from effectively processing our sadness and loss.
- We may be lacking a support structure that will allow us to fully share our losses.
- We may be escaping the losses through alcohol, drugs, or some other unhealthy diversion.
- We may have slipped into a state of depression, which hampers our ability to grieve effectively.

A complicated grief reaction isn't a sign of weakness or lack of faith. It is simply a signal that we need to change something in order to process the grief.

Several options are worth considering. This is a time to consult your physician to be sure that your body is functioning effectively. A physical disorder may be complicating the grief process. You may also need antidepressants or sleep medications for a season to help you over the hump. In addition to participation in a grief support group, you may benefit from professional counseling as well.

Again, if your sadness and grief don't diminish over time, and if your outlook on life worsens or your sadness seems protracted, seek a professional opinion. Allow this sadness to propel you into action. It's time to seek additional help.

Godly Sorrow Leading to Repentance

We've seen that feeling our sadness helps us cope with loss and move forward with our lives. But the Scriptures tell us that even more is in store for us when we experience a godly sorrow over sinful actions.

> Now I rejoice, not that you were made sorry, but that your sorrow led to repentance. For you were made sorry in a godly manner, that you might suffer loss from us in nothing. For godly sorrow produces repentance leading to salvation, not to be regretted (2 Corinthians 7:9 NKJV).

The apostle Paul tells us here that we can realize our sinfulness and turn away from practices of sin. With a heart challenged by conviction, we feel intense sorrow. We feel sad about this conviction, and it leads to repentance—a turning away from the sinful habits that have enslaved us. We feel a new sense of freedom!

Godly sorrow that leads to repentance is profound. We have erected fortresses around our secret actions, telling ourselves that no one will find out about them and that no one is being hurt by them. We tell ourselves lies in order to cope with and maintain our sinfulness.

In a moment, however, our defenses can be shattered. Something triggers a response, and we are forced to face the truth—our lives are not working. We had believed the lies, we had settled for half-truths, we had worked hard to convince ourselves that small sins don't amount to anything. But now, in this moment, sadness overwhelms us. A healthy, life-giving sadness. We have an opportunity to embrace the sadness and shamefulness of actions we know to be wrong.

Coming face-to-face with our sinful actions, we feel sorrow because we catch a glimpse of the pain we cause God. The psalmist David cried out in sorrow, "Against you, you only, have I sinned and done what's evil in your sight" (Psalm 51:4). Godly sorrow touches our hearts at a deep level. In this place of remorse, we attempt to understand what our sin means to God and to our own soul. We understand that God looks at the thoughts and intentions of the heart, and we sense that He is touching and healing us in this secret place.

This is a tremendous opportunity for emotional decision making. In this moment, we experience repentance—*metanoia*—a change of mind and purpose. We no longer think the same thoughts, feel the same feelings, or do the things we used to do. This godly sorrow is a renewing, transforming experience because it leads to repentance and forgiveness.

Thankfully, we don't stop with simply turning away from our wrongfulness—we are touched, cleansed, and forgiven. This is the heart of repentance. It is also a wonderful example of using sadness to bring about miraculous change.

11

Searching for the Missing Peace

*What we achieve inwardly will
change outer reality.*

Otto Rank

We lead very busy lives. Many couples work long hours and then spend their "free time" transporting children to soccer matches, gymnastics, and other activities. Not surprisingly, many of us are frazzled by the end of the week. We flop into the weekend, hoping for emotional recovery and at least a glimpse of peace. In addition to family obligations, many of us struggle to keep finances in check, perform routine home maintenance, and then, if we're lucky, squeeze out a few hours for an occasional workout. Spiritual activities are boxed into slivers of time when available.

We try to do it all, so it's no wonder our emotional and spiritual lives often take a backseat to the tyranny of the urgent. We've got to get the plumber out to fix that clogged drain, tend to that overdue roof repair, and shop for those must-have items for the kids.

Christie and I lead a normal life. She attends school five days a week in Seattle, a 30-minute ferry ride and an hour's drive from our home. After finishing her interior design degree, she can look forward to working full-time. I have offices in three cities, and sometimes I feel as if I'm passing myself coming and going along Interstate 5. In stolen moments of time, I write books and try to catch up with Christie and my life.

One night not long ago, we decided to sit together on the couch and just talk.

"What a concept," she said. "An evening to get to know one another! I'm not sure I remember what that feels like."

I don't mean to paint a depressing picture. Christie and I chose our lives, and they are full and rich. However, we occasionally acknowledge the price we pay for our hectic lifestyle. That evening, we wondered about a slower pace, more friendships, the opportunity to spend time boating.

Just this morning we sat on the patio of our Bainbridge Island cottage with cups of coffee, watching sailboats skimming across the water, the Seattle skyline framing the picture. Then we took a brisk walk on the beach before I sat down to write. Moments like this remind me of what I am missing.

If you are at all like me, your life is full to the brim. You have too much month left after the money is gone and too many chores left at the end of the day. Your spiritual life is squeezed into nooks and crannies. You feel proud if you're able to block out a full hour for a Sunday morning church service.

These full lives do have benefits, but most certainly they have drawbacks as well. Our days are bloated with activity and thin with time for reflection and peace. When asked what people want more of, the common answer is time and peace. The two often go hand in hand.

This chapter is about learning from our experiences and emotions so we can find and develop peace in our lives. Utilizing our emotions to move us in the direction of more godly and peaceful lives should be one of our highest goals. In the following pages we'll learn how our emotions can propel us toward that goal.

No Time or Space for Reflection

Recently I spoke with Karla, a busy insurance agent who seems to thoroughly enjoy her occupation. She is good at it and is quite successful.

Karla is a professional acquaintance. In her late forties, she is attractive and dresses modestly, but she seems a bit pinched. Her speech is clipped and rushed as if she is always in work mode. She carries her portfolio with her wherever she goes.

Karla sat next to me at a business luncheon and shared how she and her husband had separated for three months because of alcohol issues and problems concerning "irresponsibility." She shared how, over the years, she involved herself in work as a way to compensate for his absences.

"I like my job," Karla said. "When he started staying after work to spend time drinking, I decided I might as well put my time to use. Now with the kids grown, there isn't much else for me to do."

Karla stated that her work was very rewarding, but it had gradually taken her away from her faith and perhaps even her marriage. In years past she had been active in her church. Now, with her busyness at work and her marriage problems, she has pushed away from involvement at church. In recent years, she has felt as if she stepped into a revolving door and can't get out. Her increased activity—which left her with no time for reflection, solitude, and renewal—has contributed to her fatigue and irritability. She misses the peace she knew in years past.

As a step toward reclaiming some balance in her life and setting aside some quiet time with the Lord, Karla dedicated a small enclave in her house to spiritual purposes.

I was intrigued with the idea.

"I don't understand," I said. "Is that all you use the space for?"

"Yes," she said. "I keep my Bible there. I have pictures of people I pray for on the walls, and I do my journaling there. I want to get back in touch with feelings I turned off a long time ago."

"Is this a desk and chair, or is there more to it?" I asked.

"It's a built-in desk, and I've anointed it to the Lord. When I show up, it feels like He's already there, just waiting for me to arrive."

I wasn't sure what to think about this, but the idea was unique. After all, the Old Testament talks about Moses being instructed to build a tabernacle as the dwelling place of God, serving as a place for worship and the offering of sacrifices. Why not create a "tabernacle" in our homes dedicated to God? Why not have a place designed for the sole purpose of meeting with God, much as we use our living rooms to entertain friends?

From a psychological perspective, I could see the value of having a setting designated as a holy place where Karla could meet with God. If she prepared her heart for meeting Him, much as we do when entering the sanctuary of our church, and reserved this space for this purpose, it could help facilitate a powerful experience.

"So how is it working?" I asked.

"It's a remarkable thing," she said. "I don't know if it's because my heart is ready for worship or because He already inhabits this nook in my home. But I've been able to quiet myself and think through a little more clearly what God wants me to do about my marriage and my life. I'm believing God will work on my heart and my marriage."

Mindfulness

Karla has done what I've been promoting in this book—she has used her emotions to make critical decisions in her life. She had been feeling increasingly irritable, tense, and void of peace, and she made a decision to change things. She felt alienated from God and was determined to create a space for Him in her life. This decision is now reaping wonderful rewards for her—primarily a sense of peace about her marriage and future.

In a small way, I've encouraged a similar activity for anyone coming to me for counseling. I've challenged them to set aside time every day to journal and listen to their feelings and to the movement of God in their lives. I want my clients to develop an attitude of mindfulness so they are no longer content to simply react. Instead, they will begin to notice how they act.

The difference between reaction and action is huge. When people react to every situation and circumstance in their life without ever stopping to determine if that is the way they want to behave, they are functioning at a very primitive level. Conversely, when people watch for patterns in their life, and then measure their responses against goals and ideals they've established for themselves, they are far more likely to grow and change in a positive manner. They are also far more likely to step out of destructive, chaotic patterns of living and move into a more peaceful mode.

I tell my patients to monitor how the week goes. I tell them to be mindful of which situations make them feel better and which make them feel worse. When they observe and note the feelings they have, they begin to recognize patterns.

I want my patients to do far more than monitor their feelings, however. I want them to *learn* from them. I want them to be mindful of their actions and the impact these actions have on their emotions. Likewise, I want them to be mindful of their emotions and note how they affect their actions. Finally, I want them to be sensitive to how God might be interacting with them during certain situations.

Restless Minds

Although I have been singing the praises of using emotions for decision making, we sometimes need to temporarily separate ourselves from our roiling feelings and restless minds. This is necessary because making good decisions with an agitated mind is nearly impossible.

Although some decisions demand immediate action, most allow us time to consider the situation. The old saying "Muddy waters become clear when still" reminds us that we can rarely figure things out when we're working overtime. This is why agitated minds often produce impulsive decisions. Healthy, positive solutions come to us when we're quiet, undisturbed, and reflective.

I have found that I cannot discuss serious matters late at night. In fact, Christie and I have an agreement that when I'm tired, cranky, and sorely in need of sleep, we won't address any problems that need our attention. To force an issue when I'm at my worst does no justice to the issue, to Christie, or to myself. Thus, we leave important decisions for the morning hours.

There is more than a grain of truth to the notion of "sleeping on it" when trying to solve a problem. After wracking our brains all day to formulate a solution to something that is bothering us, a good night's sleep can often help us see the challenge more clearly and find the answer.

But what are we to do when we have a cacophony of emotions jousting for position in our brains? Desiring a quiet mind is one thing, but attaining it is quite another.

Here are a few ideas I've discovered for calming the mind so that we can better understand our emotions and make more effective decisions.

Letting Go

Western culture promotes working on problems. We seem intent on thinking and wondering and tinkering until we've solved the issue. We're like a dog with a bone, and after a while it's unclear whether the dog has the bone or the bone has the dog.

The fact of the matter is this: We sometimes need to "let go and let God." We must learn to give our problems over to the One who is more capable of solving them. Rather than whiling away hours of our lives on useless cogitation and agitation, we can train our minds to do what is within our power to solve and then, through faith, release what remains to God.

In this regard, the Serenity Prayer by Reinhold Niebuhr is very powerful: "God, grant me the serenity to accept the things I cannot change, the courage to change the things I can, and the wisdom to know the difference."

This prayer is similar to the words of Solomon:

"Trust in the LORD with all your heart and lean not to your own understanding; in all your ways acknowledge Him, and he will make your paths straight" (Proverbs 3:5-6). The apostle Paul said it another way: "Do not be anxious about anything, but in everything, by prayer and petition, with thanksgiving, present your requests to God. And the peace of God, which transcends all understanding, will guard your hearts and your minds in Christ Jesus" (Philippians 4:6-7).

One of the surest paths to peace is to cast our cares on the One whose shoulders are best able to carry them. Still, we are often tempted to take back our concerns. Melodie Beattie reflects on this struggle in her book *The Language of Letting Go*:

> After identifying our needs, there is a next step in get-
> ting our wants and needs met…We let them go, we give
> them up—on a mental, emotional, spiritual and physical
> level. Sometimes this means we need to *give up*. It is not
> always easy to get to this place, but this is usually where
> we need to go…If I then embark on a plan to control or
> influence getting that want or need met, I usually make
> things worse. Searching, trying to control the process does
> not work. I must, I have learned to my dismay, let go.[1]

Meditation

Again, letting go is often easier said than done. I must let go when everything in me—my emotions and thoughts—are clamoring for attention. This is a time for consideration, not action. A time for stillness, not helter-skelter impulsiveness.

Meditation is one of the most powerful mechanisms for slowing our thoughts. New Age gurus have caused Christians to be skeptical of meditation, but immersing our minds on the Word of God (as opposed to emptying our minds or meditating on some mantra) surely has a place in the Christian's arsenal of tools. Consider the words of the psalmist David: "Blessed is the man who does not walk in the counsel of the wicked or stand in the way of sinners or sit in the seat of mockers. But his delight is in the law of the Lord, and on his law he meditates day and night" (Psalm 1:1-2). The psalmist also prayed that the meditation of his heart would be pleasing to God (Psalm 104:34).

David wasn't the only one who used meditation. After Moses died, God encouraged his successor, Joshua, with these words: "Do not let this Book of the Law depart from your mouth; meditate on it day and night, so that you may be careful to do everything written in it. Then you will be prosperous and successful" (Joshua 1:8).

This kind of meditation didn't involve emptying the mind, but rather focusing on Scripture. David (and we can assume, Joshua) chose a passage of Scripture and mulled it over, much like a cow chewing its cud. They recited the Scripture, considered it, and reflected upon it, letting it speak to their heart.

These actions brought a stillness these leaders needed to make the monstrous decisions they had to make in battle. Meditation led them to peace. Quieting the mind in this manner softens our tumultuous feelings, stills our bodies, and brings the Word of God to bear upon our situation. It is one way to find the missing peace in our troubled lives.

Silence

If white noise and restlessness create tension that leads to poor decisions, silence helps us settle frayed nerves and endless chattering in our minds. Silence allows us to slow down and listen to what God might have to say about a situation. Again the psalmist instructs us: "Be still, and know that I am God" (Psalm 46:10).

In a world filled with cell phones, iPods, pagers, instant messaging, television, movies, and radio—not to mention the visual noise of billboards, neon lights, and stop-and-go traffic—silence seems about as attainable as a winning lottery number.

How can one find peace in this raucous world? Karla has the answer. She became intentional about creating a space and time to be free from distraction and to be alone with her thoughts, her feelings, and God. During that time, there are no cell phones ringing, no televisions blaring, and no radios screaming at her.

In recent years, periods of quiet have become increasingly important in my life. Thankfully, my wife shares this same desire. We shudder as we make our weekly trek to Wal-Mart for supplies, knowing we'll encounter traffic congestion, masses of people, eye-popping deals too difficult to refuse, shopping lines with even more "deals" at the checkout counter, and yes, noise! Always plenty of noise.

At times, we wonder if we're becoming boring people. A perfect evening most often consists of snuggling together on the couch and reading a good book or magazine. As we watch the moon rise over the Cascade Mountains, I feel my emotions and spirit settle into a long, relaxing "ahhhhhhhhhh."

Research has shown that I'm not out of the mainstream. Experts are now encouraging people to seek increased silence, both from outside and within, to find more satisfaction and happiness. Too many of us have become anesthetized to the incessant racket of our world even though this same din takes its toll on our level of inner peace.

Solitude

Just as surely as we seem unable to escape noise and the attention grabbers that surround us, many of us seem to have an equally low tolerance for solitude. Being alone is akin to being stranded on a desert island without your iPod and cell phone—unthinkable! We're really frightened of being alone. For that reason, we fill our social calendars, keep ourselves busy to the point of exhaustion, and surround ourselves with television, radio, and anything else that might distract us from ourselves. Of course, these same distractions usually create noise and tension and draw us further from our goal of inner peace.

But solitude has many benefits once you get over the withdrawal from the noise in your life. Solitude brings clarity to situations, heightening our awareness of our emotions and allowing us to make even better decisions.

On our recent trip to Mexico, I went for a solitary run every morning, culminating in a few minutes alone on the beach, listening to the pounding Pacific surf. Like most people, I seem to experience some things only through stillness and solitude. There, alone on the beach and free from myriad distractions, my emotional life gained a greater clarity. I thought about decisions facing me—the goals I have as a writer, the concerns I have for my aging parents, the pride I feel for my sons, the hopes I have for my marriage.

Anthony Storr writes in his bestselling book *Solitude: A Return to the Self* about the benefits of solitude:

> The capacity to be alone is a valuable resource when changes of mental attitude are required. After major alterations in circumstances, fundamental reappraisal of the significance and meaning of existence may be needed. In a culture in which interpersonal relationships are generally considered to provide the answer to every form of distress, it is sometimes difficult to persuade well-meaning helpers that solitude can be as therapeutic as emotional support.[2]

He's right. As an emotional helper, I've been quick to promote support but slow to suggest quietness and solitude. But I've found solitude increasingly beneficial in my life.

Simplicity

My final suggestion for quieting the mind is simplicity. As a card-carrying, dyed-in-the-wool accumulator, simplicity is another lesson I've learned the hard way.

Simplicity seems to be a lesson that is chasing me, rather than vice versa. Just as certainly as I'm moving toward more quiet in my life, I'm also being drawn inexorably to simplicity.

The modest Bainbridge Island cottage that Christie and I acquired is decorated sparingly, and because of its smallness, anything out of place quickly becomes clutter. Here, with little to generate "noise," I am able to write effectively, think clearly, meditate firmly, and gain clarity in my emotional life. The simplicity of our 1930s, 1000-square-foot cottage is perfect for emotional decision making.

In his wonderful book *Everyday Simplicity,* Robert Wicks describes the focus of simplicity:

> It is on dropping things so we can have "space" within us where egoism doesn't live, greed is absent, and preconceived notions don't block our clear, appreciative vision of life...We need an inner sanctuary where the pesky voice of need is quieted and we can simply be. Without such space, we become too distracted and preoccupied to be awake to what is both important and real in life.[3]

In perhaps the Bible's quintessential passage on simplicity, Jesus offers these incredible words of instruction:

> Therefore I tell you, do not worry about your life, what you will eat or drink; or about your body, what you will wear. Is not life more important than food, and the body more important than clothes? Look at the birds of the air; they do not sow or reap or store away in barns, and yet your heavenly Father feeds them (Matthew 6:25-27).

A Challenging Journey

As you have by now gathered, the quest for the missing peace is not an easy one. You will encounter many obstacles along the way if indeed you even decide to embark on the journey to seek peace.

In my clinical practice, people commonly tell me they want peace in their lives but then refuse to do what is necessary to find it. They want the absence of anxiety, discouragement, and strife but don't want to take steps to gain tranquility. One young man in particular epitomized this struggle.

Stephen was a hardworking attorney who had passed the bar exam several months earlier. After years of intense study, he was now beginning to enjoy the fruits of his labors.

Obviously fit and well-toned from an ambitious exercise regimen, Stephen wore a custom-tailored suit to his first appointment. He then shared how the hours he'd spent studying for his law degree were nothing compared to the hours he was putting into his work. Stephen told me that as a newcomer to his firm, he was expected to hustle and churn out billable hours. But doing so left him little time for his young family or church.

Work and exercise were his life, and subsequently he felt little peace. He exercised, in fact, primarily to rid himself of the tension created by the 80-hour workweeks.

Stephen and I discussed his out-of-balance life. We discussed his growing disdain for the legal practice because of its demands, the increased tension in his marriage, and the nagging feeling of guilt and sadness that were plaguing his spiritual life. Stephen was an emotional, anxiety-filled wreck. He wanted the peace he had known at earlier times in his life and sought counseling to find it.

I applauded Stephen for seeking counsel. Having listened to his own account of anxiety and discouragement, he knew something needed to change. However, his resolve ended there. After a few sessions, when I suggested Stephen consider the prospect of a lower status in the law firm, he cancelled further appointments, choosing to discontinue counseling and continue on his dead-end path toward turmoil.

Having lived the life of a workaholic, I have a pretty good idea why he stopped coming. He had worked long and hard to complete a rigorous program and obtain a law degree, and now he was earning plenty of money. He drove a fancy new car and was buying a fine house in the most prestigious part of town. He could afford anything he set his mind on. And with that came power. Weighing his desire to get ahead with his quest for inner peace, he folded. He compromised, believing the lie that we can have it all without consequences.

Did Stephen really want peace? Absolutely.

Was he willing to give up some things for it? Yes and no.

When it came right down to it, he wasn't willing to make the sacrifices necessary to achieve the balance he so desperately needed in order to find peace in his life. Sadly, his emotional life will have to suffer even more before he is willing to make the changes that will bring him peace.

Just as surely as success comes at a price, so does peace. Giving up our desire to accumulate things and choosing a life of simplicity are not easy. Turning down the din of this world and opting for silence, coming face-to-face with ourselves when we're alone in solitude, trusting that God meant it when He said we don't need to worry and that He would take care of our needs...none of these actions come naturally.

Finding the missing peace may not be a simple journey for you. You may experience many uncomfortable feelings on your quest. The path to peace will lead you across some important bridges and through some distressing territory.

Stephen wasn't ready to make the journey.

The Author of Peace

Imagine the setting: Jesus is meeting with His disciples after His crucifixion and resurrection. The bewildered disciples had had no time to process these events, and now, only days later, He stood before them again.

Remember that the disciples had disappointed Jesus. They had failed to sit with Him during those grueling hours in the garden of Gethsemane, and Peter had denied even knowing Him. They had failed their beloved friend and Savior.

Guilty, sad, and confused, they were probably prepared for the lecture of their lives. And Jesus had a right to be pretty steamed over their actions.

But there were no accusations, no threats—only compassion. Jesus came to them and reassured them, breathing the Holy Spirit into them. He then voiced these loving words: "Peace I leave with you; my peace I give you. I do not give to you as the world gives. Do not let your hearts be troubled and do not be afraid" (John 14:27).

But even these words are a bit confusing.

Jesus tells us He offers peace but not the kind the world offers. What kind of peace is He offering? The world suggests that peace comes with a hefty bank account, lots of friends, a well-paying job, and a large, beautiful home. The world says we should seek peace from ourselves—in our achievements, in our status and power, in our self-confidence—but these things fizzle and fade, leaving us as anxious as before, still searching for the missing peace.

When accomplishments cease to hold their promise, when status and power fail to deliver their guarantee, when self-confidence will no longer buy peace, we realize that trust in God and His love for us is what truly sustains us. When guilt resulting from our myriad failures plagues us and when tensions from the workweek drain us, we can hear His words and encouragement—"Peace I leave with you."

Jesus offered peace to the disciples but didn't force it on them. This is true for us as well. His peace is available to us, but we must reach out and take it. We must pass up the fleeting peace that tempts us and reach out to grasp the real thing.

I distinctly recall a time many years ago when my cousin, Reverend Jim Sundquist, a Covenant pastor, offered the following benediction:

"Grace and peace to you from God our Father, through our Lord Jesus, the Christ, in whom we have all that we are and all that we're ever going to be, in a world through which our God's grace shall have no ending. Amen."

I was nearly reduced to tears as Jim held his hand forward toward the congregation. Was my soul really so thirsty for a passing of the peace? Did my cousin have supernatural power to offer it? Or, having fully participated in the peace Jesus offers, was Jim simply honoring his responsibility to pass the peace? Having discovered the missing peace, he was responsible to help others find it. Just as we have been forgiven, just as we have been offered peace and reconciliation, we are to offer those gifts freely to others as well.

In these times of inner and outer turmoil, accompanied by emotional restlessness, I wish for you the supernatural gift of peace—not the worldly kind, but the kind given by Jesus.

"Grace and peace be yours in abundance through the knowledge of God and of Jesus Christ our Lord. His divine power has given us everything we need for life and godliness through our knowledge of him who called us by his own glory and goodness" (2 Peter 1:2-3).

12

Making Room for Joy

*Your joy is sorrow unmasked. And the
self-same well from which your laughter rises
was often-times filled with your tears.*

RENÉ DESCARTES

In the midst of everyday emotions and the stresses and struggles that fill our lives, we have many reasons to be grateful.

I sometimes can't see the blessings of life, especially when anger, fear, and pain are clamoring for attention. Yet making room for joy is always essential.

This isn't the same as wearing rose-colored glasses or denying reality. We often have reasons to be discouraged in life, but we have many more reasons to be joyful. We must simply be sure to make room for that joy.

Here's a case in point. As I write this chapter, I'm an expert witness in a challenging child custody case. An emotionally battered woman and her attorney approached me to share testimony about domestic violence and the impact it has on victims and their children. Despite being vulnerable and afraid, she courageously plans to tell the story of her abuse in front of people who might doubt her motives and veracity.

I will be in the same courtroom, and while not personally involved, I'll feel hesitant as well. I will undoubtedly be lambasted by the opposing side, which will seek to discredit me and highlight any inconsistencies.

This is part of the work I do for a living, and it truly is *work*. I worry about whether I've covered my bases and made the most accurate and compelling argument possible. I fret about what the attorneys will think of me and my skills. I wonder if I'm as prepared as I need to be.

In the meantime, I want and need to live a balanced life. In the midst of cases like this and the other challenges of a private counseling practice, I must create space for my wife, my recreational hobbies, and my spiritual life. I must literally seek and create opportunities for joy to come into my life.

In a world fraught with political tensions and a nation torn by rivaling factions, I choose to let joy shine into my life. I make this choice gladly. Each of us can find something to complain about, but we must not allow these issues to consume us. Large and small pleasures can bring us joy if we create room for them. "Gloom and doomers" are on every corner, but I purposely choose to allow more favorable emotions into my awareness.

What Is Joy?

Have you taken your relational joy temperature (RJT) lately? Many of the emotions we've discussed are painful and dissatisfying, such as sadness, discouragement, and resentment. Now we will flip the coin over and consider other emotions that lend balance to our lives.

Many marriages are dying because husbands and wives are unaware of their RJT. They have accumulated truckloads of emotional debris and walled themselves off from one another and from joy. Avoiding painful emotions by temporarily escaping or avoiding difficult encounters, they now face a joyless marriage. Having walled off certain pains, they've also walled off joy, happiness, and surprise.

But what is joy? How can we know if we've lost it or if we're experiencing it fully? To know the answers, we must first understand this delightful emotion.

Webster's defines joy as "the emotion evoked by well-being, success, or good fortune or by prospect of possessing what one desires." Its synonyms are *delight* and *gaiety.* It is further defined as a state of happiness or cause of delight.

In most cases, we experience joy when we feel great delight or happiness about something especially rewarding or satisfying.

As I look back on my own life, several moments of unbridled joy stand out in my mind. I was especially enveloped by joy at the birth of my first son. Having planned this pregnancy, my wife and I studied the latest, greatest methods of birthing—Leboyer and Lamaze. But I could not possibly have prepared myself for the exquisite delight I felt when Joshua entered the world.

During those first few hours on November 14, 1977, I was aware of only one thing: I loved this little boy so very much. Never one to think babies were adorable, I felt differently about this little guy. He was stunningly beautiful with rosy cheeks and deep blue eyes. All the cares and worries of life evaporated when I looked at him.

Two and a half years later, we were blessed with another blond-haired, blue-eyed boy—Tyson. Again, I was flooded with that same raw emotion and pure joy I'd experienced when Joshua was born. I had to pinch myself to believe such wonder could enter my life. During these precious moments of bliss, everything was right with the world.

In addition to these extraordinarily joyful events in my life, I have many small, daily doses of joy. The surprise phone call from Christie telling me about the highs and lows of college life, the early morning jog along the harbor, the steaming latte at the Blackbird Café, where I catch up on the latest happenings in town and watch people. The Blackbird's community bulletin board, with scraps of paper vying for space and selling everything from guinea pigs to guitars, always delivers two thimbles of joy and a big, light, airy smile.

The Weight of Our Story

The lightness of joy contrasts with the weight of other emotions. The story of our lives has weight. Your days, like mine, are likely filled with tensions, struggles, and emotional challenges. Everything we do creates corollary emotions—some pleasant and some challenging. Every sharply spoken or received word affects us; every personal tragedy plays on our minds. Even seemingly small losses carry emotional weight.

Your story consists not only of your day-to-day life but also of your lifelong history. The places you've been, the people you've seen, the mistakes you've made, and the wrongs done to you all carry emotional meaning. Your feelings are tweaked every day, yet in the midst of this tweaking—where emotions can roar to life at a moment's notice—we must find a space for joy. We must create a positive attitude so that joy can find a suitable home.

I recommend that we keep our emotional slates clean by living close to our emotions. This can be challenging. We must monitor our emotional reactions, explore the beliefs that feed into those emotions, and of course, attempt to make the best decisions based on this invaluable information.

In addition to managing our routine issues, we must also deal with the weight of our history. Many people have so much trauma and pain in their past that living in the here and now is very difficult. Some people trudge through life dragging a ball and chain of unprocessed emotions. Joy cannot survive long in this climate.

Whether you have trauma in your past that haunts you or you simply feel overwhelmed by the mounting emotions that accompany day-to-day living, creating room for joy may be more difficult than you might think. Melodie Beattie speaks to this issue in her book *Finding Your Way Home*:

> Each of us has our own story to tell about things that happened, people who did things to us or didn't do things for us, and the emotions that were generated in our hearts

and souls. From betrayal to sadness to rage to feeling
miffed, frustrated, hopeless, or unloved, we each have a
list of emotions that we're carrying around that still have a
charge locked in our energy field. This list is affecting our
lives, our beliefs, and the clarity of our vision.[1]

Our issues, many accumulated simply from living with fallible
parents, are often buried alive. The accompanying emotions create a
barrier between us and the possibility of joy. Like so many bricks in
an emotional wall, we're closed off from the pleasures and delights
of life.

Dan Allender, author of *The Healing Path,* understands the challenges many face in opening themselves to the possibility of being
hurt. Having been injured badly in the past, many people retreat,
erecting walls between themselves and a world that may bring them
harm. However, this insulation severs them from the possibility of
joy as well. We need to rediscover our desire to reach out again to the
world, with all its possibilities for elation and disappointment.

"Openness involves a hunger for life," Allender says. In order
to really experience the fullness of life, he explains, we must "savor
greater joy in spite of the inevitable sorrow. We can dance, eat, sing,
drink, talk and party with more joy if our hearts truly grasp God's
perspective on our past, the purpose of our future, and the passion
we are to embrace in our present."[2]

Coming Alive

Having experienced years of burying their feelings, many people
feel a vague sense of dullness. Although not depressed or devastat-
ingly sad, they often feel numb. They experience no significant lows
or highs. Joy is a foreign emotion to them.

To feel the highs of life, we must be willing to experience the
lows. To experience joy, we must be willing to come alive to the daily
losses and sadness we have described earlier in this book. To discover
the exhilaration that is ours in the Christian life, we must be willing

to experience the discouragement, anger, and betrayal as well. We cannot have one group of feelings without the other.

You may have decided to bypass the unhappiness, choosing instead to deal only with the practical aspects of life. After all, what can one really do about losses that happened in the past? You may still be unconvinced that we must feel everything that comes with our lives. But that is how we create room for joy.

We need to understand that avoiding our emotions is impossible. We cannot deny our feelings—we can only postpone or disguise them. At some time, in some way, we'll have to experience them. In one form or another, our emotions will come out. The cost of denying them is akin to emotional death. Separating ourselves from our painful emotions separates us from our joy—and from God because He speaks to us in part through our emotions.

Sue Monk Kidd, in her book *God's Joyful Surprise,* shares her struggle in unearthing her emotional debris: "I had to remove the rocks blocking my life in order to create space for God to enter and take residence. That meant effort and discipline."[3]

I invite you to participate in some emotional archaeology as a way to come alive to your emotions. It is the only healthy path. I'm not advocating that we allow our emotions to rule us. But our feelings *will* control us as long as they're outside our path of emotional decision making. Once we acknowledge, feel, and understand them, we can make healthy decisions. We can come alive emotionally—and this is a sure path to making room for joy.

Roger and his wife traveled to Washington State to work with me in a Marriage Intensive, during which I met with them several hours a day over three days. Our goal was to chip away at the conflict that had created barriers to intimacy and joy in their relationship. During these sessions, we examined their emotional roadblocks—often stemming from years of buried feelings—to create room for joyful relating.

I talked with both Roger and his wife, Tricia, several times over the phone prior to their arrival, and I knew Roger wasn't excited about spending three days with me.

"Nothing personal," Roger said during one phone conversation. "I just have never put much stock in counseling. I think we should be able to work out our own problems."

"But you haven't been able to do that, have you?" I said.

"Not exactly," he said. "But it's not that bad, at least to me."

"So why do you think Tricia is pushing for this?" I asked. I actually had talked to Tricia and knew she felt like this trip was a last-ditch effort to save their marriage. Things were desperate as far as she was concerned. Much of her concern centered on her husband's lack of emotional availability.

"I'm not really sure."

"C'mon, Roger," I said. "Tricia has surely talked to you about this. What has she been telling you?"

"She says I work too hard and that I'm no fun anymore. She says I'm boring. She wants to add more spice to our marriage. Says she wants to do more things, go more places. She's tired of sitting home, I guess."

"And do you think she has a point?" I asked. "She told me she feels like she has to do all the emotional work in the relationship. She has to encourage the talking, and she feels like the burden is on her to create the happiness. Does that sound familiar?"

"She works at it a whole lot more than I do, that's for sure."

Getting Roger to acknowledge the desperate condition of his marriage was challenging. This was the reason Tricia had sought my services.

Listen to Tricia's perspective, which she shared with me prior to their trip to Washington.

"Roger is a nice man. I still love him. He's been a great provider. A good, Christian man with a strong faith. I appreciate that about him. But he's emotionally dead. He doesn't have many lows, and he certainly has no highs. There's no joy left in our marriage, and even though we're in our fifties, I'm too young to live like this. We need to reawaken our marriage. I want some new experiences. It seems like we're sleepwalking, and I'm tired of it."

Roger had a particularly difficult time hearing these words. He seemed to believe that if things weren't bad—at least as he saw them—then they must be good. He falsely believed that he could ignore conflict and deny the problems that he and Tricia were having. He had a hard time understanding that he needed to express all his emotions and that doing so could actually create a powerful bridge between him and his wife.

We focused on the honest expression of emotions, getting rid of patterns of avoidance and denial, and increasing expressions of warmth and intimacy. It wasn't easy work because their destructive patterns were entrenched. Yet both Roger and Tricia noticed many positive changes during our sessions. Roger identified some buried feelings of hurt he had hidden from Tricia, and he discovered that he tended to isolate himself rather than talk about them. He also agreed to begin dating Tricia again and taking some trips with her to add some spice to their marriage.

Roger and Tricia also agreed to add small, daily doses of joy to their marriage by noticing positive things about each other and bringing positive, joyful conversation to their relationship. They agreed that a big smile and friendly greeting were simple pleasures that were easy to give to one another.

Fortunately, they came alive in time to head off the death of their relationship. Not all couples are so fortunate. Counselors have noticed a national trend of middle-aged women ending marriages because they are no longer willing to live in lifeless, joyless relationships. After living without joy for so many years, they often take drastic measures to find it. They understand that coming alive is the antidote to the problem. They're willing to feel every emotion from being miffed to feeling frustration and grief. They realize that not expressing emotions creates barriers between mates and limits the possibility of joy.

Waiting for Joy

People have said that we cannot seek joy; it comes to us. Many believe that joy, like happiness, is more a by-product of a life well-lived than something we pursue. Delight comes to those with the right frame of mind—the proper mental and spiritual attitude.

However, I do believe we can actively create conditions whereby joy is likely to be a frequent visitor rather than a long-lost friend.

To create space for joy, we must know what it looks like. Although we cannot actively seek it, we don't have to sit idly by, waiting for it to arrive. We must achieve a precious balance.

What might joy look like in your life? What situations seem to evoke delight? Where and when is joy most likely to happen?

Recently, Christie and I had dinner with our friends Robin and Mike, the Realtors who sold us our island cottage. Mike and Robin talked passionately about their recent trip to France. The enchanting travel abroad wasn't the only thing that excited them, however. They were surprised that the French landscape and architecture had touched their hearts so deeply.

"I've got to tell you," Mike said, leaning forward as he spoke, "that there is something absolutely splendid about the limestone cottages in France. They are so beautiful, efficient, and solid. There's a sense of permanence. Robin and I stayed in one cottage overlooking the ocean, and I didn't want to leave. She had to force me out of there. I felt so at peace that I just wanted to let the place soak into my bones. I was in heaven."

"Sounds like you found something very special," I said.

"Boy, did we!" Mike said. "I want to take what I discovered there and replicate it here as much as possible."

"How are you going to bring that experience back with you?" I asked.

"I'm looking into using stone indigenous to this region to build our retirement cottage. I appreciate plants and materials that are friendly to the environment. I want the next house we build to make sense, and that excites me. I want a place that will bring me peace and happiness."

Mike and Robin had discovered something powerful on their trip to France—a sense of place and a type of structure that had meaning for them—and they vowed to bring part of it back with them. They were determined to hang on to the experience and nourish it. They weren't content to wait for joy—they actively sought ways to create it.

While Mike and Robin found joy in their travels and their future plans, something else about them attracted me. Both had a zest for life and simple pleasures. Robin enjoys gardening and creates a tranquil atmosphere in her home. Mike enjoys cooking and reading about current events. Both are well-read and interesting people—and interested people. They seemed to enjoy asking Christie and me about our latest treasures and pleasures as well.

A Vision for Joy

Many people wait passively for joy because they're unfamiliar with the feeling and may not know precisely what they're waiting for. They know emotional pain but they don't know emotional happiness and joy.

A particularly challenging aspect of my counseling practice is helping people see beyond their current worries, to see the gift in their struggles. Everyday gifts are hidden in the midst of life's difficulties. I never want to diminish my clients' present pain, but I want them to experience the fullness of their emotional life.

This can be a bigger dilemma than you might think. Filled with sadness, anger, and discouragement, my clients struggle to set positive goals, to establish conditions where joy might appear. For some, you'd think I was a snake-oil salesman.

"How can I imagine a brighter future?" they ask. "I don't know what one day is going to hold, let alone what the next will bring."

"But you can imagine what you'd like to see happen in your life," I say, brimming with confidence and enthusiasm that is lost on many of them.

Many try to envision a brighter future, but deep inside we both wonder if they'll follow through. They struggle to take hold of the visions that are so small and vulnerable. I can envision a brighter future for them, but they aren't sure they can make it their own. They've lived too long with their harsh realities, waiting for some distant joy to come to them.

"I don't think joy will come to me," they say with obvious discouragement. And sure enough, it often doesn't. Not because it can't but because they won't make room for it.

"I told you so," they say when things fall apart, fulfilling their expectations. "I've never been happy. I'm not happy now and won't be happy later."

"Whether you think you're going to have a good day or a bad day, you'll be right," the saying goes.

Having a vision for joy is a critical element in finding and experiencing this wonderful emotion. Rather than having an emotion and then making a decision, we can work in reverse in this instance: We consider what circumstances might exist in order for joy to arrive, change our behavior accordingly, and then anticipate that joy will enter our lives. We alter our attitude and create an opportunity for joy to exist.

Sailing has always brought me delight. Nothing is quite as exhilarating as being on a sailboat, seeing the sun shining brightly off the water, and sharing conversation with good friends. Whenever I conjure this image, I drift back to wonderful days on Puget Sound, headed for some new and exciting harbor for lunch.

As I write this chapter, I'm sitting at my desk and peering enviously at the sailboats, tugs, barges, and luxury craft sailing in and out of Elliot Bay near Seattle. I have a vision of someday owning our own 30-foot sailboat and mooring it close by at Bainbridge Island Marina. Sailing has brought me much joy in the past, and I'm ready to invite it into my life over and over again.

On a smaller scale, I also envision joy in the gathering of the men's group at my church. Each Friday morning, at the unwieldy hour of six thirty, we gather to discuss the upcoming sermon over hot coffee and fresh donuts. The men's smiles and easy laughter continue to bring me back. I carry the camaraderie and companionship with me and eagerly anticipate it all week. These friends bring me joy.

Being Open to Life's Possibilities

Having a vision is one of the ways we help ourselves experience joy. But it's not the only way. Another is being open to life's possibilities, as F. Washington Jarvis explains in his book *With Love and Prayers:*

> In addition to long-range vision, there is a critical second ingredient to happiness: namely, approaching day-by-day life affirming the possibility of happiness in all its events…To find happiness in the midst of daily life—in our school work, or job, or marriage—we must approach them positively, affirmatively.[4]

This concept is not new. Brother Lawrence practiced finding the presence of God—and the joy that accompanied it—in the mundane routine of washing dishes. Mother Teresa found happiness in working with the poorest street people in Calcutta, India. If we cannot find joy among the many possibilities that everyday life has to offer, we may not be able to find it at all.

We can find joy in the oddest places when we are open to new possibilities. What if we approached our relationships, our jobs, and our daily routines with the attitude—even the assumption—that we might discover joy? What if I decided that every situation had something to teach me, something to strengthen me, something to make me a better person? With that attitude, joy might be a more frequent visitor rather than a stranger.

Let's consider some of the everyday possibilities for joy. As you scan this list, be wary of the critic within who says, *That's ridiculous. That can't possibly bring me joy. I need larger, grander things in my life.* Instead, believe that you can find joy in simple settings like these:

- a nature walk, discovering new shapes and forms in the handiwork of God

- a museum, viewing awe-inspiring works of art, including some that evoke new and different emotions

- an alternative worship experience, like a Taizé service, a revival, or a service at a new church

- a new form of prayer, such as lectio divina, reading one small portion of Scripture over and over

- eating your meal slowly and deliberately, appreciating and tasting every bite

- a new friendship, or inviting people from different age groups to your home and appreciating their unique lifestyles, attitudes, and interests

- a visit to a new city, walking slowly through a new, nearby town and looking carefully in the windows

- serving at a homeless shelter, allowing yourself to escape the routine of your life and enter fully into the lives of others less fortunate

- a new form of celebration, allowing yourself to act silly and laugh more often

The list could go on and on. The common denominator is being open to possibilities. Joyful people celebrate life. They actively try to replicate positive experiences and maintain an awareness of what brings them joy, and they also invite new experiences into their lives and accept the unexpected events that occur naturally.

My wife has a knack for being open to life's possibilities. She rarely labels an experience as bad, but rather sees the possibilities in every situation. If we miss a ferry that would have gotten us home earlier, she sees an opportunity for a dinner out. If we can't attend a party, she gets excited about the opportunity for us to spend an evening alone. For Christie, every troubling situation is filled with opportunity. Subsequently, joy is a frequent visitor in her life—and now in mine.

No Strangers

Making room for joy almost always involves allowing other people to touch us emotionally. Most often, people who are isolated are separated from humanity and from the opportunity to care for others and be cared for.

People are rich with differences, so they often make us stretch ourselves to be more accepting of possibilities. We can be enlivened by those who are strange but not necessarily strangers.

I'm excited to see the resurgence of the notion of community. More and more cities are developing "city centers"—also known as "third places"—mass transit and parks and other gathering places. Coffee shops flourish in part because of our growing desire to reverse the trend toward isolation created by suburbs. We want to connect with one another again, allowing ourselves to touch and be touched by others.

People lacking joy are often too wrapped up in themselves. They take themselves too seriously, and that seriousness is antithetical to joy. Laughter, surprise, and delight are best shared in groups. The joyful person doesn't think less of himself; he just thinks of himself less!

Perhaps as you read this chapter you are feeling sadness because you are estranged from important people in your life. You have a son or daughter who no longer speaks with you; there are factions at work, where rivalry and competition are more important than cooperation; you attend church but don't allow anyone to get close to you.

Intimacy is a wonderful promoter of joy. Consider the possibility that you need to be reconciled with someone with whom you have conflict. The apostle Paul says, "If it is possible, as far as it depends on you, live at peace with everyone" (Romans 12:18). There is little as sweet as fellowship with others.

Joyful people have learned the art of being at home with others. The Scriptures call this *koinonia*. The gospel story is largely about groups of people gathering together and sharing their lives. Here, in community, we are called to bear one another's burdens (Galatians 6:2).

Joy in the Faith

Any careful reading of Scripture reveals the truest source of joy for Christians: their faith. Amazingly, creating room for joy doesn't seem to involve changing external circumstances—it involves simple faith.

"Convinced of this," the apostle Paul says, "I know that I will remain, and I will continue with all of you for your progress and joy in the faith, so that through my being with you again your joy in Christ Jesus will overflow on account of me" (Philippians 1:25-26).

Joy in Jesus Christ.

Paul is saying that we can find meaning and purpose in our relationship with the Lord Jesus. In this dynamic, growing, life-changing relationship, our emotional and spiritual DNA changes, and we are transformed from within.

Many of us are mired in our daily struggles, but Paul reminds us of our eternal reward. "No eye has seen, no ear heard, no mind has conceived what God has prepared for those who love him" (1 Corinthians 2:9). God has dreams that are bigger than our dreams. He has hopes for us that extend far beyond our hopes.

Our relationship with Jesus Christ is a primary source of our joy. The Scriptures tell us, "But the fruit of the Spirit is love, joy, peace, patience, kindness, goodness, faithfulness, gentleness and self-control" (Galatians 5:22). This fruit of the Spirit is the spontaneous work of the Holy Spirit, not something we contrive. We don't grit our teeth and hope for the best. We don't hold our breath and then peek into the mirror to see if we've changed yet. We're changed to be more and more like Him. As we allow the Spirit of God to work in us, we will experience joy.

If you are struggling with raw emotions in this life, and if the challenges of daily life get you down, that's okay. Remember, Jesus cares about every aspect of your existence. He promises to bring joy through your relationship with Him (John 15) and to carry you through your trials. He even promises you joy in the midst of your afflictions (Romans 5:3-5).

Perhaps the greatest source of joy in my life is this promise: "And we know that in all things God works for the good of those who love him, who have been called according to his purpose" (Romans 8:28). All of my struggles and every one of my feelings—God can use them for good, and that brings me immense peace and joy. To know that God will transform even my worst experiences and elicit good from them is very reassuring.

Knowing this allows me to lean into difficult circumstances. Knowing that good will come of situations that at first make me angry, sad, discouraged, or even bitter creates space for me to give thanks and invite God in so I can experience joy in the midst of my trials.

What is the status of your faith life? Have you had experiences that have caused you to distrust the hand of God in your life? Perhaps you need to loosen your grip on your circumstances and invite God to show you how He wants to make room for joy to flow into your life once again.

Trust Him, He'll do it.

Epilogue

Listen to Your
Heart for a Change

*Life does not accommodate you,
it shatters you…Every seed destroys its
container or else there would be no fruition.*

Florida Scott-Maxwell

I love new cars. I love their smell, the fresh paint, and the shining bumpers. Most of all, I relish the gadgetry that seems to improve with each new model.

My VW Beetle came with a CD player, a dash indicator that tells me when it's time for a tune-up, a low gas alarm, and a super-whoopee radio with a "seek" button so I can tune into the nearest station.

Cars can be very impressive, but have you ever considered that we have a pretty sophisticated instant emotional feedback system built into our bodies? It's called *the heart*.

Our physical heart performs important bio-physiological functions, but metaphorically, our heart has long been considered to be the seat of our emotions. The heart offers us critical feedback. Like a warning light in our cars, the heart offers emotional information so we can adjust appropriately and make important decisions.

Our heart reflects our passions, registers when we've been hurt, and resonates what is important and beautiful to us. When we are confused about what is missing in our lives or what course of action we need to take, we can listen to our heart as we consider the possibilities for change.

The heart doesn't always offer feedback that we like. It can tell us when we are spiritually distressed, but that doesn't mean we automatically know what is wrong or what to do about it. But if we consider the situation, prayerfully reflecting on our emotions and thoughts, we can usually arrive at a reasonable course of action.

Science has discovered many of the heart's physical functions. Similarly, we can continue to identify the role of our emotional heart. Consider the value we place on the heart and the language we use when describing emotions connected with it.

- She has a cold heart.
- He is a leader with heart.
- He was heartless in his actions.
- We must never lose heart.
- She had heartfelt emotions.
- He's a man after my own heart.
- I know it in my heart.
- He won her heart.

The Scriptures support the centrality of our heart as a source of emotional knowledge. It is the storehouse for our innermost thoughts and feelings.

- "Love the Lord your God with all your heart and with all your soul and with all your mind and with all your strength" (Mark 12:30).
- "I will give you a new heart and put a new spirit in you;

I will remove from you your heart of stone and give you a heart of flesh" (Ezekiel 36:26).

- "Then you will look and be radiant, your heart will swell and throb with joy" (Isaiah 60:5).

Our heart plays a critical role in helping us understand our thoughts, motives, and emotions.

The Critical Balance

As the prophet Jeremiah noted, the heart can be deceitful. How do we know we can trust it?

I believe balance is the key.

I have written this book because we are confused about our emotions. Either we repress our emotions so we can get on with life or we react to each daily occurrence, creating a roller coaster of emotional highs and lows.

Either extreme is detrimental. The Mr. Spocks among us are hardly any fun, being so cold and detached that we wonder if they have a heart at all. Having a relationship without emotions is like hugging a refrigerator.

At the other extreme are those who exhaust us by overreacting to every situation. At times, they may be warm and cuddly, but they also demand that we accompany them on their emotional thrill ride. Exhaustion sets in, and we must push away to catch our breath.

Clearly, we must find a balance, and the key to balance is not to react to our emotions or repress them, but to release them. When we attend to our emotions, offering them a safe place to incubate until ready for expression, we no longer keep a cork on our bottle of feelings about everyday events and past traumas that still strive for attention.

We *release* our emotions by listening to our heart.

Throughout this book I've suggested keeping a journal as a way to listen to your heart and to find the rhythm of your life.

This rhythm helps you determine what's missing and what needs to change.

Just this morning I was reading Psalms and journaling. I read Psalm 57 very slowly, which is the way I prefer to absorb the Scriptures. Psalm 57:2 settled into me. "I cry out to God Most High, to God, who fulfills his purpose for me." What purpose does God have for me? What purpose is He fulfilling in me?

I'm still uncertain about all the purposes He has for me, but I was able to come up with a list of recurring themes and possibilities:

- He is opening more doors for my writing.

- He is giving me opportunities to speak to larger audiences.

- He is giving me greater opportunities to minister to couples and individuals experiencing emotional pain.

- He is leading me to cut back some of my clinical hours in the office.

- He is giving me opportunities to teach classes on relationships at our church.

- He is leading me to give more of my time to service in our community.

As I reflected on these, I considered another psalm of David: "Delight yourself in the LORD, and he will give you the desires of your heart" (Psalm 37:4).

I wrote this in my journal: "Thank You, Lord, for the opportunities to write. I so enjoy this and would like to do more of it in my life. Please open and close doors to the kinds of writing You want me to do and the topics You feel need to be written."

I am immensely grateful for the opportunities to write, but my journaling includes another theme. I release and explore my emotions. Here's yesterday's entry: "Christie and I have been talking about our schedules and anticipating slowing things down this summer. Lord, I'd like Ryan (my associate) to fill in more for me in my practice as he seeks to increase and expand his practice."

I've been edgy and anxious at times with my busy schedule. I've been envious of others who have had the guts to slow down and live simpler lifestyles. In my heart, I want to do the same. I want to be courageous enough to step out in faith and allow our finances to fit our simpler lifestyle. I also pray to lessen my desires to accumulate more stuff that I don't need.

Overwhelming Emotions

The only times my emotions become unmanageable are when I *react* after a season of *repression*. How can I calmly listen to my feelings when they're screaming at me? How can I create an atmosphere where I'll freely *release* emotions in healthy ways and make decisions accordingly?

Just last evening I had to practice what I've preached in this book. I received a phone call from a woman at the state's attorney general office. She wanted to ask questions about a court case I will be involved in this coming week.

"The attorney for the other side is brutal," she said. "She's going to go after your opinion in your psychological evaluation. She completely disagrees with you and will try to discredit you in any way possible. You need to simply answer her questions and not get caught in her antics."

I felt an immediate rush of emotions—anger, anxiety, and even dread.

As the day wore on, I felt increasingly apprehensive. Having recently finished another grueling case, I wasn't prepared for yet another encounter with an overly aggressive attorney. Feeling anxious and overwhelmed, I wondered about my decision to become a forensic psychologist.

Anxiety is our best friend and our worst enemy. Sue Monk Kidd, in her wonderful book *When the Heart Waits,* talks about the importance of seeing crises as opportunities. She explains that anxiety and other feelings are flashing lights on the dashboard of our psyche, indicating that we must pay attention.

> An internal uprising could be as simple as a vague sense of restlessness, some floating disenchantment, a whispering but relentless voice that says, There has to be more than this. Why are you doing what you're doing? Or the uprising may take the form of stress, burnout, a chronic sense of exhaustion, inner voices desperately trying to tell us something.[1]

Just when I thought I was okay, my anxiety grew. My skin crawled, my thoughts raced, and I began to feel dread about this court case. I didn't want to be drilled, attacked, maligned, and discredited. My attempts to silence my emotions by distraction had failed, and by necessity I now had to face them. They simply weren't going away.

Attending to Our Emotions

Sitting down to journal again, I heard the front door open. I breathed a sigh of relief, knowing it was my wife—and she'd be willing to debrief with me and help me make sense of my emotions, which she gladly did.

I shared my apprehension and anger at having to defend my evaluation in court. I *released* my frustration and fear, my anxiety and discouragement. Christie listened, spoke lovingly to me, and rubbed my feet as I vented my emotions. We agreed that my immediate need was for rest, to take a walk, and to find time later that day to play. We also revisited the ongoing questions I've had about my schedule and whether I want to continue taking on so many court-related cases. The lights on my dashboard were flashing, and I needed to listen to my emotions and make healthy decisions from them.

The goal is not to repress our emotions, nor is it to be reactively driven by them. We need to listen to our hearts and, if we're willing to do so, determine what action we need to take to restore emotional balance to our lives.

The heart is a wellspring of emotion, and we must guard it. But the heart is also a source of critical information. In our hearts we evaluate what is vitally important to us. In our hearts we know truth.

Changing Our Thoughts and Attitudes

Beneath our clamoring emotions are thoughts and attitudes that drive those emotions. Beneath my anxiety about court were thoughts of wanting to impress people, fear of public ridicule, and the ongoing pressure of maintaining a steady referral base for my private practice, including those from attorneys and social workers. This often involves accepting referrals I might not prefer to take.

As I take note of the flashing lights on the dash of my psyche, I need to examine them in relation to Scripture. Underlying much of our anxiety and discouragement are attitudes and beliefs that contradict God's Word.

The Scriptures challenge us to "renew our minds" so that we can resist conforming to cultural trends (Romans 12:2). The Scriptures encourage us, "Do not be anxious about anything, but in everything, by prayer and petition, with thanksgiving, present your requests to God. And the peace of God, which transcends all understanding, will guard your hearts and your minds in Christ Jesus" (Philippians 4:6-7).

The apostle Paul teaches that we must turn everything over to God. Having prayed to Him with our requests, we are promised peace and the wisdom to find the answers to our disturbing circumstances.

Troubling emotions usually flow out of troubling life situations and troubling thought processes. Invariably, if we look beneath the surface of our anxiety and distress, we'll uncover patterns of living and thinking that need change. Such is certainly the case in my life, and I believe you'll find it to be true for you as well. As I've listened to my heart and my emotions, I've gained a greater clarity about how I need to live my life.

Balance remains a key challenge in my life. Christie and I are more committed than ever to remain active in our church, and I attend the Friday men's group. We are determined to exercise regularly, eat right, and enjoy our friends more. These activities fuel the natural renewing of our minds, making us more able to meet the emotional demands of work.

Catharsis

We've come a long way in this book. We've examined the value of tending to our emotions. We've discussed the role that anger, sadness, hurt, and bitterness can play in helping us create positive changes. We've focused on the need to create a space for emotional pain in order to create room for joy as well.

You now face another opportunity—the potential for *catharsis*— expressing years of pent-up feelings, wounds, and losses. As we become more intimate with our emotions, loosening the cap on years of feelings, we give ourselves the opportunity for catharsis.

Melodie Beattie, in her book *Journey to the Heart,* poignantly explains how emotions become stuck within us.

> Just as splinters can get embedded in our body, old emotions and beliefs can act like toxins and become embedded in us, too. We may have picked up residue along the way—beliefs we didn't consciously choose, feelings we weren't safe enough to feel, toxins from the world around us.[2]

Perhaps we don't mean to bury our emotions. It just happens because we haven't created a space for them to simply *be.*

Perhaps you can relate to Julia Cameron, who writes in *The Artist's Way,* "But we are nice people, and what we do with our anger is stuff it, deny it, bury it, block it, hide it, lie about it, medicate it, muffle it, ignore it. We do everything but *listen* to it."

She is referring to anger, but she could just as easily be talking about fear, sadness, bitterness, resentment, or any number of feelings that we judge as inappropriate and worthy of being stuffed back into the powder keg, where they are sure to explode at some later date.

> Anger is meant to be listened to. Anger is a voice, a shout, a plea, a demand. Anger is meant to be respected. Why? Because anger is a map. Anger shows us what our boundaries are. Anger shows us where we want to go. It lets us see where we've been and lets us know when we haven't liked it…Anger is to be acted upon. We are meant to use anger as fuel to take the actions we need to move where our anger points us.[3]

Most of us walk around with a residue of anger and hurt clinging to our souls like a foul odor. Over the years we have repressed it again and again, but now we have the opportunity, by paying closer attention, to listen to the wisdom of our emotions and make the proper adjustments. We don't need to react, but to release. We don't need to take impulsive action, but to experience the freshness of letting go of old hurts, wounds, and anger, and in the process, to make room for delight. In fact, when we allow ourselves the healthy release of emotion, we decrease the likelihood of an explosive or passive-aggressive reaction.

Do you keep a fierce grip on the container of your emotions? It's time to let go and loosen your grip, allowing the cathartic release of emotions to lead to appropriate decisions and changes in your life. An emotional catharsis may include crying at losses, expressing anger at violations of your boundaries, or feeling and sharing disappointment at possibilities you haven't attained. As you release emotions, you may discover or uncover even deeper wounds and emotions seeking expression. This is a journey leading to emotional release and health.

Being Thankful for Our Emotions

As we come to the close of this book, can you thank God for your emotions and the lessons you're learning from them? As you've walked through this book, have you been able to become friendlier with your feelings? I hope you've learned how each and every emotion, from pain and sadness to joy and delight, can be instructive on your path toward peace.

Let this be our prayer:

> Thank You, Lord for creating us with a mind, will, and emotions. We have been created in Your image, so we know that these emotions are no mistake but are an integral part of our likeness to You. Help us to balance our emotional lives with godly reason and to make healthy decisions based on what they reveal to us. Amen.

Notes

Chapter 1—Emotions and the Heart of God

1. Cited in Jeffrey MacDonald, "Rabbi's legacy of spirituality and activism is guiding light," *USA Today*, January 31, 2007.

Chapter 2—Naming and Embracing Our Emotions

1. Raphael Cushnir, *Setting Your Heart on Fire* (New York: Broadway Books, 2003), 17.

2. Cushnir, *Setting Your Heart on Fire*, 17.

3. Pia Melody, *Facing Codependence* (New York: Harper, 1989), 92.

4. Mary Cartledgehayes, *Grace: A Memoir* (New York: Crown, 1989), 84.

Chapter 3—Emotions: Pathway to God

1. Ronald Dunn, *Don't Just Stand There, Pray Something* (Nashville: Thomas Nelson, 1991), 139.

2. Brennan Manning, *The Ragamuffin Gospel* (Sisters, OR: Multnomah, 1990), 143.

Chapter 4—Denial Is Not a River in Egypt

1. John Bradshaw, *Healing the Shame That Binds You* (Deerfield Beach, FL: Health Communictions, 1988), 74.

2. M. Scott Peck, *The Road Less Traveled* (New York: Simon and Schuster, 1978), 44.

3. Julia Cameron, *The Artist's Way* (New York: Tarcher, 1992), 80.

4. Cameron, *The Artist's Way*, 80.

5. Nora Ephron, *I Feel Bad About My Neck* (New York: Knopf, 2006), 3.

6. Robert Pasick, *Awakening from the Deep Sleep* (New York: Harper Publishing, 1992), 69.

7. Philip Yancey, *The Jesus I Never Knew* (Grand Rapids: Zondervan, 1995), 195.

Chapter 5—The Gifts of Irritability and Frustration

1. Kathryn Robyn, *Spiritual Housecleaning* (Oakland: New Harbinger, 2001), 51.

Chapter 6—Anger: The Power to Change or Destroy

1. Jon Kabat-Zinn, *Full Catastrophe Living* (New York: Dell, 1990), 210.

2. Harville Hendrix, *Getting the Love You Want* (New York: Harper, 1988), 174.

3. Hendrix, *Getting the Love You Want,* 175.

Chapter 8—Depression: Anger Turned Inward

1. Bob Murray, *Creating Optimism* (New York: McGraw-Hill, 2004), 163.

2. Murray, *Creating Optimism,* 164.

3. Don Baker and Emery Nester, *Depression* (Sisters, OR: Multnomah, 1983), 137.

4. Thomas Moore, *Care of the Soul* (New York: Walker and Company, 1992), 231.

5. Baker and Nester, *Depression,* 155.

Chapter 9—Fear: From Enemy to Ally

1. Gavin De Becker, *The Gift of Fear* (New York: Dell, 1998), 336-37.

2. Susan Jeffers, *Feel the Fear...and Do It Anyway* (New York: Ballantine Books, 1987), n.p.

3. Rhonda Britton, *Fearless Living* (New York: Berkeley Publishing, 2001), 153.

Chapter 10—Sadness: Pathway to Healing

1. Howard Clinebell, *Well Being* (New York: HarperCollins, 1992), 219-21.

2. Alexandra Stoddard, *Living a Beautiful Life* (New York: Avon Books, 1986), 151.

3. Clinebell, *Well Being,* 219.

4. Clinebell, *Well Being,* 219.

5. Robert Fulgham, *All I Really Need to Know I Learned in Kindergarten* (New York: Villiard Books, 1988), 7.

Chapter 11—Searching for the Missing Peace

1. Melodie Beattie, *The Language of Letting Go* (New York: HarperCollins, 1990), 215.

2. Anthony Storr, *Solitude: A Return to the Self* (New York: Ballantine Books, 1988), 29.

3. Robert Wicks: *Everyday Simplicity* (Notre Dame: Sorin Books, 2000), 47.

Chapter 12—Making Room for Joy

1. Melodie Beattie, *Finding Your Way Home* (New York: HarperOne, 1998), 180.

2. Dan Allender, *The Healing Path* (Colorado Springs: Waterbrook, 1999), xi.

3. Sue Monk Kidd, *God's Joyful Surprise* (New York: HarperSanFrancisco, 1989), 160.

4. F. Washington Jarvis, *With Love and Prayers* (Boston: Goodine, 2000), 47.

Epilogue: Listen to Your Heart for a Change

1. Sue Monk Kidd, *When the Heart Waits* (New York: HarperSanFrancisco, 2006), 85.

2. Melodie Beattie, *Journey to the Heart* (New York: HarperCollins, 1996), 127.

3. Julia Cameron, *The Artist's Way* (New York: Tarcher, 1992), 61.

Marriage Intensives

Dr. David Hawkins has developed a unique and powerful ministry to couples who need more than weekly counseling. In a waterfront cottage on beautiful Puget Sound in the Pacific Northwest, Dr. Hawkins works with one couple at a time in Marriage Intensives over three days, breaking unhealthy patterns of conflict while acquiring new, powerful skills that can empower husbands and wives to restore their marriage to the love they once knew.

If you feel stuck in a relationship fraught with conflict and want to make positive changes working with Dr. Hawkins individually or as a couple, please contact him at 360.490.5446 or learn more about his Marriage Intensives at www.YourRelationshipDoctor.com.

Call Dr. Hawkins for a professional phone consultation, or schedule him and his wife, Christie, for your next speaking engagement or marriage retreat.

Other Great Harvest House Books
by Dr. David Hawkins

(To read sample chapters, visit www.harvesthousepublishers.com)

When Pleasing Others Is Hurting You

When you begin to forfeit your own God-given calling and identity in an unhealthy desire to please others, you move from servanthood to codependency. This helpful guide can get you back on track.

Dealing with the CrazyMakers in Your Life

People who live in chaos and shrug off responsibility can drive you crazy. If you are caught up in a disordered person's life, Dr. Hawkins helps you set boundaries, confront the behavior, and find peace.

Nine Critical Mistakes Most Couples Make

Dr. Hawkins shows that complex relational problems usually spring from nine destructive habits couples fall into, and he offers practical suggestions for changing the way husbands and wives relate to each other.

When Trying to Change Him Is Hurting You

Dr. Hawkins offers practical suggestions for women who want to improve the quality of their relationships by helping the men in their lives become healthier and more fun to live with.

When the Man in Your Life Can't Commit

With empathy and insight Dr. Hawkins uncovers the telltale signs of commitment failure, why the problem exists, and how you can respond to create a life with the commitment-phobic man you love.

Are You Really Ready for Love

As a single, you are faced with a challenge: When love comes your way, will you be ready? Dr. Hawkins encourages you to spend less energy looking for the perfect mate and more energy becoming a person who can enter wholeheartedly into intimate relationships.

The Relationship Doctor's Prescription for
Healing a Hurting Relationship

Dr. Hawkins uncovers the hidden reasons why you may be hurting emotionally. He offers practical steps you can take to heal your hurt and suggests a plan for preventing needless pain in the future.

The Relationship Doctor's Prescription for Living Beyond Guilt

Dr. Hawkins explains the difference between real guilt, false guilt, shame, and conviction, bringing these feelings into the light and demonstrating how they can reveal the true causes of emotional pain.

The Relationship Doctor's Prescription for
Better Communication in Your Marriage

Communication is an art. Couples thrive when they listen deeply, understand completely, and validate one another compassionately. But many couples try to win arguments, not to understand each other. This user-friendly manual reveals common but ineffective patterns of relating and teaches new skills in the art of communication.

The Relationship Doctor's Prescription for
Building Your Child's Self-Image

Dr. Hawkins describes what positive self-image is, what it is not, and how to help kids develop a Christlike confidence without conceit. You'll find practical descriptions of children's psychological needs, harmful parenting habits to avoid, and constructive ways to help your children build a healthy self-image.